THE SECRET PLACE

THE SECRET PLACE

Footsteps to Finding
Your Oneness with God

ANN BEALS

The Bookmark
Santa Clarita, California

Library of Congress Control Number: 2003103951

Beals, Ann.
    The secret place : footsteps to finding your oneness with
God / by Ann Beals.
        p. cm.
        ISBN 0-930227-47-6

    1. Christian Science. 2. Spiritual life. 3.
Spiritual healing. I. Title.

BX6943.B43 2003   289.5
QBI33-1194

Published by
The Bookmark
Post Office Box 801143
Santa Clarita, California 91380

CONTENTS

INTRODUCTION

A friend once asked me what was the most profound idea that I had gathered from my study of Christian Science. Her question made me bring into focus thoughts that had been drifting about in my mind for some time. I was beginning to discern an underlying plan to the early transformation of consciousness from a material to a spiritual basis. In thinking back over the years that I had given to the study and demonstration of Christian Science, I could detect an orderly and progressive unfoldment to this work.

I had a deep love for Christian Science that began when I was in high school. I tried to understand it, but I found that my study lacked focus. Then in 1952 I had Class Instruction with Neil Bowles in Atlanta, Georgia, and I learned for the first time about the prayer of affirmation and denial – or the Christian Science treatment. This unique form of prayer gave such order and direction to my work that it marked a turning point in my life. As I studied the Bible and Mrs. Eddy's writings and worked with the treatment, I began to heal physical problems for my family and myself.

Although I found I could heal sickness, injuries and other immediate problems, the more discordant challenges in my life remained unchanged. Often when I read of the healing works of Christ Jesus and Mary Baker Eddy, I wondered, What did they know that they could heal those who were insane, lame, blind, deaf — even dead? They must have had a definite form of intelligence, a specific knowledge that was as concrete, as real, and as practical to them as the principle of mathematics was to me.

I looked at the textbook, *Science and Health with Key to the Scriptures* by Mrs. Eddy, and knew that I believed every word in it, but I did not really understand it. And so I began reading *Science and Health* and Mrs. Eddy's other writings through again and again. I read slowly, and as I read I listened from within. Every day I worked with the treatment – simply to know God better. As I devoted myself to this prayerful work I was constantly gaining some small insight into the words I read. An idea would unfold that had not been there the day before. And at the end of a day given to such study I would think — had I been doing other things I would not have gained this grain of truth that had come to me during these quiet hours alone with God.

After many years of this work, I could look back and see that I had found answers to many of my questions and I had seen many defiant problems gradually disappear from my experience. False traits of character had given way to a better disposition. My healing work was more successful. I also began to see that there was a definite form of intelligence that was the basis to spiritual healing, and as it unfolded, it was bringing about changes in the beliefs entrenched in my thinking and making my life so difficult.

In time I began to sense that my years of work had taken me through definite phases of spiritual growth that were progressive, eventually leading me to an elementary understanding of Christian Science. In this book I share this experience with you.

The last phase outlined here took place many years ago, and I am still striving to achieve a better understanding of Christian Science. But each year the way grows brighter. I am certain that this inspiration continues to unfold new insights into Truth and Love because I struggled through these early phases and laid a strong spiritual foundation within to build upon. I do believe that the human mind with its mortal beliefs and materiality must go through a purifying process similar to the one I describe before the advanced understanding of Christian Science can take us out of the mortal dream and usher us into the "secret place of the most High."

I share this experience with you in the hope that it will make your journey a little easier than my own.

Ann Beals
2003

THE SECRET PLACE
Footsteps to Finding
Your Oneness with God

by

Ann Beals

*He that dwelleth in the secret place of the most High
shall abide under the shadow of the Almighty.*

Psalms

*The "secret place," whereof David sang, is unques-
tionably man's spiritual state in God's own image and
likeness, even the inner sanctuary of divine Science,
into which mortals do not enter without a struggle or
sharp experience, and in which they lay off the human
for the divine.*

Mary Baker Eddy

The hope of deliverance from evil has always been at the
heart of Christianity. Christ Jesus foretold the coming of a promised Comforter who would teach us all things. With the discovery
of Christian Science, the promise has been fulfilled, for through this
Science, it is now possible to *understand* God, rather than relate to
Him through faith alone. Spiritual understanding reveals our oneness with the Father, and ushers us into the "secret place," where
evil is unknown and the hidden realm of Mind becomes a concrete
reality.

There is growing in world consciousness a greater interest
in spiritual things, much of it due to the discovery of an intangible or

1

spiritual realm to the universe. This new realm opens up vast horizons of the mind, and counteracts the erroneous material concepts formerly believed to be true about creation. Although this new dimension is now an established fact, the illusion of a material universe and a mortal man has become such a sophisticated structure of knowledge, that the material view still appears to be the real one. Indeed, it seems to be the *only* one. It has become so ingrained in world consciousness that it has blinded mankind to the spiritual nature of creation, and for many, it has buried their faith in God.

The false material view has failed to meet the spiritual needs of man, neither has it brought to light any final material cause for creation. Instead, the discovery of a spiritual dimension in the universe has brought the dawn of a spiritual age. It is now generally acknowledged that there is more to man and the universe than material cause and effect.

The coming of a spiritual age is the next step in the evolution of civilization. But to establish this age on a firm foundation, there must be a vision that accurately defines the nature and structure of this hidden realm. Christian Science alone supplies the complete and accurate vision for the shaping of the coming age.

The dedicated student of Christian Science is pioneering in an advanced intelligence, or new knowledge, which is enabling him to understand the spiritual dimension scientifically. Through the study of this Science, we can think our way into the realm of Mind. As we do this, we transcend our present state of mind, and find the spiritual nature of the universe and man.

It is possible to transcend the human state of mind and go deeper into the realm of divine Mind because we have been told we can do so by others who have done it. The Scriptures contain many examples of those who have cast off the veil of matter and experienced this hidden realm. In the third chapter of John, Christ Jesus said to Nicodemus, "Ye must be born again." He told his disciples, "The kingdom of God is within you."

In the Christian Science textbook, *Science and Health with Key to the Scriptures,* Mary Baker Eddy writes, "Jesus of

Nazareth was the most scientific man that ever trod the globe. He plunged beneath the material surface of things, and found the spiritual cause."

Paul also urged his followers to emerge into a more spiritual state of mind when he wrote of putting off the old man and putting on the new. In Revelation, John tells us, "I saw a new heaven and a new earth, for the first heaven and the first earth were passed away; and there was no more sea."

In *Science and Health,* Mrs. Eddy writes of John's vision, "This testimony of Holy Writ sustains the fact in Science, that the heavens and earth to one human consciousness, that consciousness which God bestows, are spiritual, while to another, the unillumined human mind, the vision is material. This shows unmistakably that what the human mind terms matter and spirit indicates states and stages of consciousness."

In *Miscellaneous Writings,* she also writes, "St. John spiritually discerned and revealed the sum total of transcendentalism. He saw the real earth and the real heaven. They were spiritual, not material; and they were without sin, pain, or death."

The promise of a transcending vision that solves the mystery of Godliness, has been with us for centuries. Nicodemus did not understand Jesus in the least when the Master told him that he must be born again. Two thousand years have passed, and Jesus' words have yet to be understood. Religions have taught about the new birth; but with the discovery of Christian Science, the hope of being born again can now be realized.

Mrs. Eddy has given us the key to the mystery of the new birth, for she too had a revelation comparable to that of John. When asked what she had experienced in 1866, when the spiritual nature of all things was first revealed to her, she said, "I saw the love of God encircling the universe and man, filling all space, and that divine Love so permeated my own consciousness that I loved with Christ-like compassion everything I saw. This realization of divine Love called into expression the beauty of holiness, the perfection of being, which healed and regenerated and saved all who turned to me for help."

Following her revelation, she was able to record it with such clarity that others can understand God as she did. Her writings explain *how* to be "born of water and of the spirit." She went much further than talking about salvation. She made it possible! She defined the spiritual realm of reality, and the true nature of God and man. She exposed matter and evil as illusions in human thought, which spiritual understanding destroys. Then she showed how to prove her statements through a new form of prayer — the prayer of affirmation and denial.

The hope of experiencing a mental breakthrough similar to those of Christ Jesus, John, and Mrs. Eddy, can be realized through the study of Christian Science. But the work of exchanging faith in God for an understanding of Him is a great challenge. It is one thing to talk *about* spiritualizing consciousness, and an entirely different thing to actually *do so.*

A Progressive Plan for Salvation

Healing works in Christian Science are proof that it is the promised Comforter. Often through impressive healings, we become dedicated Christian Scientists, relying upon it when we are in need of healing, and never deviating from the high moral standard it teaches. As we study it, we become aware theoretically of the spiritual nature of all things. We begin to understand God, and experience healing through our own prayerful work.

And yet so much is lacking. There is the promise in Christian Science of total salvation, of the coming of the kingdom of God within, and the ability to demonstrate dominion over sin, disease and death. Such advanced spiritual enlightenment does not come easily.

The door to greater spiritual understanding is found in the Scriptures and Mrs. Eddy's writings. In her article, "The New Birth" found in *Miscellaneous Writings,* she tells us, "With the spiritual birth, man's primitive, sinless, spiritual existence dawns on human thought, — through the travail of mortal mind, hope deferred, the perishing pleasure and accumulating pains of sense, — by which one loses himself as matter, and gains a truer sense of Spirit and spiritual man."

How does one lose himself as matter and gain a spiritual sense of things? How do we convert theory to fact, and exchange faith for understanding? How do we outgrow the old and put on the new? How do we spiritualize consciousness?

Even with a dedicated study of this Science, we find it so profound and so in advance of the times that it seems difficult to understand its deeper concepts. Like other students, you may have wished for a guideline or plan that would explain how to progress beyond the present level of your work in Christian Science into a more advanced understanding of it.

Actually, there is a progressive plan underlying our deliverance from evil. The purpose of this discussion is to outline the progressive stages necessary to achieve the transformation of consciousness. There are five general phases that we pass through in gradually developing a very elementary spiritual state of mind. This transformation of the mind is entirely subjective — it takes place in the consciousness of the individual.

Christian Science makes a very clear separation between truth and error, Spirit and matter, good and evil, reality and unreality. The spiritual is the real, and the material is the unreal. The purpose of the divine plan is to separate these in consciousness and replace the unreal with the real.

When I first began a serious study of Christian Science, I was aware of the new birth, but I did not understand what it involved. I read all I could find on Christian Science, but I could never find any explicit instruction as to how I could exchange mortal mind for immortal Mind. I had many unanswered questions about this. Uppermost was the uncertainty as to the actual footsteps leading from one state of consciousness to the other. How does one go from the material to the spiritual? How can it be that there is no matter when everything and everyone appears to be submerged, encased, imprisoned in matter and its laws? How can evil be nothing when there is so much sickness, lack, discord, adversity? What did Mrs. Eddy *know* that she could heal with an assurance that was far more than guesswork or some sublime faith in God? What did Christ Jesus know that he could thank God for healings before they took place? How does one find the kingdom of God within?

As far as I could tell, the way to accomplish this transformation of the inner self was not explained in detail. There was no specific plan for demonstrating the deeper truths of Christian Science. Although I did not find what I was looking for, I continued to demonstrate Christian Science to the best of my ability.

As I progressed, there were many trials to work through and challenges to meet. But there were also many healings, and I began to find answers to my questions. Slowly over a number of years, I developed an elementary understanding of Science that placed my healing work on a scientific basis. Then there came a time when I could look back and see an underlying plan to this long-term demonstration. Different phases of it became increasingly distinct. I could see that there is a logical, orderly process to entering the kingdom within — one that could be separated into distinct phases. In going through this divine plan, one could emerge out of mental darkness into an understanding of Christian Science in which God is more real than evil.

The plan which I am going to share with you is an effort to chart the footsteps which initiate the spiritualization of consciousness. I present this plan in an orderly way, but my explanation of it is over-simplified in an effort to explain as clearly as I can an extremely profound and complex experience. The five phases outlined here give only a bare skeleton of the plan, but it is a beginning — and we have to start somewhere. Through it, I hope to give you some idea as to what is involved in finding your oneness with God.

With this outline, you will see that there is far more to spiritualizing consciousness than most of us realize. It is not a simple or quick process. To find the kingdom of heaven within is not easy, but with Christian Science, it is possible.

I do not want to give the impression that I have mastered the whole of Christian Science. Far from it. I still have much to learn. But I have demonstrated the phases of this plan, and I did so almost entirely through the study of the Bible and Mrs. Eddy's published writings.

The work of transforming the inner self is an *internal struggle* to free consciousness of evil or animal magnetism, and to replace mental darkness with spiritual understanding. In this way, the mind is disciplined to think in spiritual ideas, instead of human beliefs.

Five Phases Outlined

The five phases outlined here are given as being separate and distinct, but they are actually intertwined and interrelated. They blend into one another without any clear separation or boundary between them. The focus of our work simply shifts from phase to phase as we progress. We never completely finish one phase and leave it for another. Rather, we find that we will return again and again to expand upon our demonstration of each phase.

1) The first phase is focused on learning basic Christian Science. The divine plan requires a good foundation in the terminology of Science and an understanding of the basic ideas it teaches. You must also know about Christian Science treatment — the prayer of affirmation and denial — and the importance of giving yourself a good treatment each day. The spiritualization of consciousness is accomplished through study and treatment. In this initial stage, you begin doing your own healing work.

2) In the second phase, you go beneath the surface study of Christian Science and recognize the need to obey the law of Love. Obedience to the law of Love enables you to overcome the more aggressive, ungodlike traits and beliefs that make the mind impervious to enlightenment and change.

3) The third phase is focused on understanding the unreality of matter. Mrs. Eddy states in *Science and Health,* "Matter disappears under the microscope of Spirit." To overcome the belief in matter; you handle it as mesmeric illusion. As you break the hold of this mesmerism, the spiritual nature of the universe is revealed, and matter begins to fade out of consciousness. This work brings great mental transformation to the inner self. You understand how to overcome the belief in material cause and effect, and then you see the universe and man as expressions of Mind, not matter.

4) As you are successful in seeing through the illusion of matter, you are then able to resolve one of the great fundamentals of Christian Science — *the nothingness of evil.* In the fourth phase, you come to grips with the hypnotic work of evil, or animal magnetism, claiming to produce sin, sickness, disease, lack, discord, adversity and death. You see the need to struggle with the seeming reality of evil within consciousness, until you learn to demonstrate dominion over it. In doing so, you discover that evil is nothing, and you can control and destroy it through the prayer of affirmation and denial. Once you learn this, you possess an awesome power over the belief of evil. This phase is one of the most traumatic and transforming experiences in the divine plan.

5) Following the struggle with animal magnetism, the fifth phase brings great spiritualization of thought. The veil of matter and the mesmeric influence of animal magnetism begin to diminish. For the first time, you understand that God is All-in-all and evil is nothing. This unfoldment of divine intelligence and spiritual power can come about only through a long, hard struggle with animal magne-

tism. You see now that you are in the spiritual universe of God's creating here and now! You have always been in it. In this phase, some of the least understood statements in *Science and Health* become increasingly logical, beautiful, and inspiring.

From this point on, you move ever deeper into divine reality. You discern the perfect man where mortal man appears to be. You see for the first time that man as God's likeness is submerged in a spiritual universe, living a life that expresses God's wisdom and love, governed by divine cause and effect. This understanding of God and man as cause and effect, leads to a primitive state of Christ-consciousness wherein your whole being is governed more by divine laws of health and holiness, rather than by evil's seeming laws of matter and mortality.

The five phases are progressive. Each new phase begins when you have learned the previous one enough to move on to the next. This plan gives order to your work in Christian Science. You can ask the right questions, and ask them in the proper sequence.

In this plan, I am simply sharing with you my own unfoldment. I cannot in any way outline how another's salvation should unfold. Spiritual regeneration is an individual demonstration, and no two people have exactly the same experience in the work of spiritualizing consciousness. You must decide for yourself how best to use these ideas.

A demonstration of the five phases does not mean that our work in Science is finished. We will find that, having gone through these phases, our spiritual progress continues under God's direction, as we move ever deeper into a spiritual understanding of Him. It is possible that everyone must pass through an experience similar to mine in order to reach the Christ-consciousness within. Mrs. Eddy tells us that we will experience our spiritual lessons either through Science or suffering. It is my fond hope that by exploring these phases with you, I will help you to find and follow the Science route.

An Analysis of the Mortal Dream

Advanced work in Christian Science is not concerned with treating and healing things or conditions external to consciousness, but rather with experiencing our own revelation of the spiritual nature of man and the universe. We are trying to understand God.

Before taking up Christian Science, our mind is basically mortal. World belief is made up of separate mortal mentalities which image forth collectively mortal existence. Each person embraces in consciousness a personal sense of life, and envelops himself in his own material view of things. Each human consciousness generates its own peculiar set of problems and limitations from within its own darkened mental state, which it then expresses as a false sense of life. Until this basic set of beliefs is overcome in Christian Science, the person will continue to experience the same life-style and collect around him minds of a similar nature — because his mind remains the same.

One person can do little to spiritualize the mind of another, either through prayer, advice, or instruction. Only as the individual himself goes to God — seeking help or enlightenment — can the inner self be transformed.

As we willingly yield up a mortal selfhood through our work in Christian Science, we begin to spiritualize consciousness. Through the study of Christian Science, mortal beliefs are seen to be unreal; thought is purified; the darkened, material state of mind grows increasingly less until it disappears. Eventually we do not even remember experiencing the mortal dream.

Until this transformation takes place, the human mind remains within the sphere of its own dream state from which it appears to project out into the world a mortal existence. Actually both the inner self and the outer manifestation are one; they originate within the darkened mind. This mental state never enters into the reality of God's creation. It is never conscious of the spiritual universe or spiritual man. It always remains totally confined to its own material limits.

When, in Christian Science, we become aware of our oneness with the Father, we awaken out of this darkened state of human thought, which constantly generates new problems. We no longer keep thought focused on the unreal — mesmerized with the seeming power and reality of evil. Through study and prayer, we make God so real that evil becomes nothing to us.

As we pray our way into the spiritual realm, we become aware of God as a living presence; we outgrow mortal beliefs and traits, and the misty gathering of false education and human opinions, a mortal past, a material origin, a discordant world. Pressing deeper into Christian Science — ever deeper — we find our spiritual selfhood forever one with God.

In reality, we are already in God's presence. Whether we know it or not, we are forever submerged in a universe of God's creating, with a selfhood governed by His laws, and a divine nature as His likeness. This spiritual state of being remains forever complete and undisturbed in God. Since God is infinite and eternal, we cannot be separated from His care. We may believe we are separated from Him, but in reality, we are now and forever one with Him. He never lets go of us.

Through awakening to our spiritual selfhood, we gradually outgrow the false beliefs that generate a mortal life, and so we become conscious of our true identity in God's likeness. The divine plan enables us to separate the mortal from the immortal, transcend the present state of consciousness, and then find our true selfhood in God.

The Internal Warfare with Animal Magnetism

In Revelation, John records: "There was war in heaven: Michael and his angels fought against the dragon; and the dragon fought and his angels, and prevaileth not; neither was their place found any more in heaven." The terrible events in John's account of Armageddon have left the impression that a great universal holocaust, a war to end all wars, is inevitable. There have been prophesies of the end of the world for centuries — a time when good people would go to heaven and receive their reward, and evil people go below and get what's coming to them. And I suspect we're all rather confident as to where our place will be if such a time comes!

Do we assume that this great warfare will be objective? Is it not possible that John was describing the *internal warfare that must be waged with the animal magnetism claiming to be within us?* Perhaps the correct interpretation of Revelation would show that Armageddon is *completely subjective.* It takes place entirely in the inner self. In the textbook, Mrs. Eddy writes, "Every mortal at some period, here or hereafter, must grapple with and overcome the mortal belief in a power opposed to God." This implies that there is before us a great struggle to be born again through the overcoming of the animal magnetism that claims to be in our own consciousness.

If Armageddon is a subjective warfare with evil, *then salvation is also a subjective experience.* No one can be kept out of the kingdom of God, for it is entered from within; but neither can one person do this work for another. Each must think and pray his own way into heaven. God alone unfolds the spiritual ideas which bring about this transformation. The coming of the Christ-consciousness takes place entirely within the inmost thoughts.

As you press against the boundaries of your mind and strive to demonstrate spirituality, you discover depths of consciousness you didn't know were there. Salvation is not a mystical experience or an instantaneous transformation that eventually overtakes us somewhere in time. It is a slow, divinely-ordered, learning process which comes through a series of subjective breakthroughs into the realm of reality. Through this schooling in spiritual things, you overcome the animal magnetism within that is presently claiming to be in you and to be you.

The work of overcoming animal magnetism within consciousness is a point that is not stressed enough in Christian Science. As a rule, when we think of handling animal magnetism, we see it as something "out there," something apart from us, perhaps attacking us and giving us much to meet. We say we need to protect or defend ourselves against aggressive mental suggestions external to the mind, coming through the thinking of others or as a world belief.

But in fact, if another's thoughts are claiming to harm us, there is always some error in our thinking that lets in such malpractice. If this were not so, we would be the helpless victims of the negative thoughts and emotions of others. But as consciousness is spiritualized, we are divinely protected from malicious mental malpractice, because there is no animal magnetism within our own consciousness to let it in and cause us to react to it.

While an understanding of malpractice is an essential part of Christian Science, it is far more important to recognize the animal magnetism that seems entrenched in consciousness as our own mortal thoughts and emotions. *It is the animal magnetism within that must be handled and overcome.*

It is sometimes difficult to convince someone that he needs to reform his own thinking, especially if he is a good person — honest, reliable, kind, intelligent, capable. So often the good person sees no error in himself to reform. If he is living Christianity to the best of his ability, or is a dedicated Christian Scientist, he honestly believes he has no need to change. But the fact is, even Christian Scientists are still thinking in a mental atmosphere filled almost entirely with animal magnetism. The fundamental structure of the human mentality is comprised of erroneous material knowledge and a mortal personality.

Human goodness cannot be substituted for spiritual consciousness. It does not prevent discord, adversity, age, disease, or death. We may be well versed in the letter of Christian Science and have healings from time to time, and still be only theorizing about it,

13

making absolute statements that we cannot prove, and dealing in platitudes that are meaningless. Human goodness leaves the inner structure of thought, or what appears to be our mortal personality, for the most part unchanged.

We learn that *salvation does not come through human goodness.* Salvation starts here; but to gain dominion over all evil, we must let Truth uncover and cast out the animal magnetism within which claims to be our human personality.

What seems to shut us out of our oneness with God? — the seeming reality of evil and matter. Animal magnetism has mesmerized consciousness so deeply and is so common in world thought, that we think in it effortlessly. The human mind is a solid mental medium made up of good and bad elements that seems impervious to change. It is educated in universal beliefs of matter and mortality, and shaped by the prevailing mental atmosphere. As a rule, there are no drastic changes in either the inner self or outer expression of this human selfhood throughout one's lifetime, because mortal mind cannot detect and destroy the animal magnetism within that is shaping the outer life.

Until Christian Science is introduced into consciousness, we think almost entirely in mortal mind — a mental darkness with little or no spiritual understanding. As evil's hold on us goes unchallenged, the mind seems submerged in varying degrees of human beliefs. In this darkened state of mind, evil seems more real and powerful than God. Until we are educated to handle animal magnetism, we have no sure means of defending ourselves against its hypnotic influence.

In order to spiritualize consciousness and gain dominion over evil, we must do battle with the animal magnetism *within* until we exercise such fearless dominion over it that we can reduce it to nothingness. In doing this, we dis-abuse the human mind of its influence. Until we can demonstrate this dominion, evil seems to be solid conviction in the inner self. We cannot be free of this influence until we de-mesmerize consciousness through study and prayer in Christian Science.

Evil's Resistance to Being Destroyed

If we call evil "nothing" and ignore it, we are not handling it in Christian Science. When we undertake an internal warfare with evil, we find that evil cannot be labeled "nothing." At this stage of our experience, it is a seeming power that tenaciously resists its own destruction. This resistance makes our prayerful work very challenging. Mrs. Eddy once told a student, "Animal magnetism is powerless — but you must declare against it as though it had ALL POWER." She also tells us in *Miscellaneous Writings,* "Christian Scientists cannot watch too sedulously, or bar their doors too closely, or pray to God too fervently, for deliverance from the claims of evil."

In every phase of the divine plan, animal magnetism resists mightily its own destruction. Unless you recognize what it is doing, it handles you without your knowing it. It is subtle, devious, cunning. It comes in many guises. When you try to study and do metaphysical work and you have to fight off a deep, almost hypnotic sleep, you are encountering evil's power to stop your metaphysical work. If animal magnetism cannot put you to sleep, it will distract you, intensify your problems, cause you to procrastinate or ruminate, make you feel guilty that you are not busy doing something more productive. Whatever the reason for delaying the work, animal magnetism is the cause of it. Your first internal fight with evil is with this resistance. If you give up and do not learn to handle this resistance, you will eventually be forced to do so through suffering — and I really don't think you want to go that route!

If you don't give up, if you stay with the work until you break down this tendency to sleep, if you outwit the devious distractions of evil, and refuse to procrastinate, you will begin to have some dominion over it. Then you will see why it can be called nothing. Its seeming hold on consciousness is broken. You are learning how to control it; it can no longer control you.

Each time you are successful in detecting and destroying any belief of animal magnetism within, you free your consciousness of it. Mortal mind begins to thin out, making space in consciousness for God's ideas to unfold. As error is destroyed, it does not leave a vacuum within. Spiritual ideas unfold to replace it, and the inner self is permanently transformed.

FIRST PHASE: LEARNING TO PRAY

You begin your journey into the secret place by learning to do successful metaphysical work in Christian Science. The study of Science is a very serious undertaking, and as Mrs. Eddy tells us, "demands absolute consecration of thought, energy, and desire."

Having become established as a student of Science, your next step is to become thoroughly educated in its teachings, and accomplished in giving a good Christian Science treatment. You need to make it your business to learn as much about Christian Science as you can. This education comes through study and prayer.

Mrs. Eddy tells us, "Desire is prayer." Then the question arises, what do you desire? Do you pray for healing, or for something you want or need? When such prayers are answered, you have proof of God's goodness. But there is a higher motive for prayer that eventually brings you into the secret place. *You can pray simply to know God better.* You can yearn to understand Him. With this divine purpose as your motive, God becomes the focal point of consciousness, and you are receptive to His thoughts. Through long, quiet hours alone with God, you can concentrate on spiritual things and learn from Him the realities of being. When prayers are focused on this one goal, you come to feel the warm, gentle presence of His love, and discern His thoughts unfolding as new insights into the divine reality of all things.

When a pure desire to know God motivates prayer, the study of Christian Science is not a duty that you force yourself to fulfill. It is a holy time in which you establish a rapport with the

Father and begin demonstrating your oneness with Him. Through study and prayer in Christian Science, it is possible to understand God. It is not easy, but it is possible.

Understanding God begins with reading the Scriptures and the writings on Christian Science, especially Mrs. Eddy's works. Reading is in itself a form of prayer. Yearning to understand these writings, you read and ponder the ideas for their spiritual meaning. Through this humble asking for "an understanding heart," you are receptive to God's thoughts. Then He can reach you, and slowly unfold the ideas that teach you the deeper meaning of Christian Science. This spiritual state of mind is then manifested in healing, and you learn to heal through your own metaphysical work.

Reading always remains a basic requirement in Christian Science. We never outgrow the need to read and ponder the Scriptures, Mrs. Eddy's writings, and the more advanced works on Christian Science. Through daily study, we learn the letter of this Science, its terminology, and the fundamental truth it teaches. It is important to read the more profound works on Science which have been written over the past century. [These advanced writings on Christian Science are available through The Bookmark, Post Office Box 801143, Santa Clarita, CA 91380.]

When you begin this study, Christian Science may seem difficult, because you are not yet accustomed to thinking in spiritual ideas. Works on divine metaphysics may appear abstract, theoretical, impenetrable. But reading them introduces into thought spiritual ideas. When the mind is focused on God, truth is active in consciousness. Continual reading will gradually unfold the hidden meaning of the Bible and *Science and Health.* Sometimes there is resistance to reading *Science and Health* from cover to cover because it is a difficult book to understand. But how are we going to understand it, if we never read it? By reading it from cover to cover time and time again, we grow familiar with the profound truth that Mrs. Eddy has given us.

Reading Christian Science is essential if you are going to demonstrate dominion over animal magnetism. But simply reading

Science is not enough. In fact, some students of Science who have been doing this for years, are still not too successful in demonstrating it. Simply to study this Science as a religious, intellectual, or philosophical exercise, does not convert the letter to spirit. You must also understand and use the treatment — the prayer of affirmation and denial.

Reading Christian Science is preparation for giving a good Christian Science treatment. The treatment is a unique form of prayer. It does more than petition God for help and healing. It is a prayer of action, in which you take the initiative and affirm with conviction the spiritual facts about God and man, and deny with equal conviction all the beliefs of matter, mortality, and animal magnetism. In this way, you pray intelligently, for you are putting out of consciousness false mortal images and replacing them with the spiritual facts of being.

The treatment is a simple but very effective method of praying. You can begin by affirming God through the seven synonyms — Mind, Spirit, Soul, Principle, Life, Truth, Love. This affirmative prayer unfolds an understanding of God as All-in-all. Next, you can affirm man in His likeness, and the universe as His creation, by relating them to the synonyms also. Thus you understand God as spiritual cause and man and the universe as spiritual effect. Next comes the denial part of treatment. When you have this truth established in consciousness, you are able to deny the power and reality, the very existence of evil, mortality, and matter with conviction. You can aggressively, even vehemently, deny all forms of animal magnetism, and this gives you dominion over them.

Reading and study, combined with treatment, are the key to entering the secret place. Reading educates you in the letter of Christian Science, and the treatment converts the letter to spirit. In this way, you think and pray your way into heaven.

The prayer of affirmation and denial is so basic to the demonstration of Christian Science that I have written a book on it entitled *Christian Science Treatment: The Prayer that Heals.* I urge you to study this book, along with my booklets, *Animal Magnetism* and *Scientific Prayer.* They explain how to work with the treatment. You must be accomplished in the treatment in order to go through the other phases outlined in this book. Christian Science treatment is the means through which you commune with God most effectively. It turns faith into understanding and theory into fact. It is the most powerful and the most advanced form of intelligence in the world today.

Importance of Study and Prayer

Spiritualizing consciousness comes about through daily study and treatment. The elements of the human mind do not change without an effort on your part, for the human mind of itself cannot create, or even properly speculate over a spiritual condition it has never known. Neither can an understanding of God be contrived or manufactured, using the mind's present mortal state of thought. Intellect or an opinionated view of what Science means and how it must unfold, is no substitute for the unfoldment of God's ideas. Inner transformation comes in the heart of prayer.

The purpose of treatment is to annul the animal magnetism within which obstructs the unfoldment of God's ideas. *Just as all spiritual transformation takes place subjectively, animal magnetism's claim to obstruct spiritual progress also takes place subjectively.* We unconsciously consent to this mesmeric control in one way or another. Without daily study and treatment, we continue tilling the same mental ground with little or no progress. Blind faith in God does not handle animal magnetism. Analyzing mortal mind does not handle it. Study and treatment alone bring the radical change within which frees us of it.

Study and prayer are necessary because animal magnetism is basically what we now seem to think in. It is the format or medium of the mind. Unless we are aware of its resistance to the truth, we do not see how it operates in consciousness as our own

19

thoughts and emotions. It would seem that people and circumstances outside of our consciousness are preventing us from praying. We may seem trapped in discordant, painful, limiting conditions over which we have no control. But our lives are our thoughts objectified. These conditions are actually the animal magnetism in our own consciousness objectifying itself as a mortal life.

Through prayerful work, you can bring about a chemicalization within that brings error to the surface and destroys it. Powerful metaphysical work is necessary to de-mesmerize consciousness of the claims of animal magnetism — a mortal personality, a material universe, an evil force opposing God. Through strong, constant denial of evil, and strong, constant affirmation of truth, you free consciousness of all that is unlike God.

You need to study and pray so earnestly because spiritualization of thought involves learning a totally different state of mind — one completely unknown at this time. It is an advanced intelligence that you do not have yet, an intelligence that is the opposite of human knowledge and beliefs. Revelation is the appearing of this advanced intelligence. As you silently pray, as you are receptive to God's thoughts and listen from within, you generate a subjective flow of spiritual ideas. This inspiration simply unfolds. At one time these ideas are not known to you, and then they are.

The treatment brings the truth into direct contact with the animal magnetism in consciousness in such a way that the truth annihilates the error and replaces it. This metaphysical work brings about a chemicalization through which mortal mind dissolves, and consciousness reflects the divine Mind. You then think and live in a new dimension of the mind, and there is no return to old thought-habits. You should treat your mind each day until you achieve some new insight into God. Then, however small this insight may be, these moments of unfoldment will gradually transform the whole of consciousness.

Spiritual regeneration is a learning process. You develop an understanding of God as you might develop an understanding of art or music or engineering. Just as the human mind changes with continual education in academic subjects, it also changes with constant schooling in the Word of God.

Through study and treatment, you come to think in spiritual facts as easily as you now think in material beliefs. This work molds and remolds your mental atmosphere with ever new and progressive insights into Truth and Love, and this brings about a completely different state of mind.

All spiritual transformation takes place in the heart of consciousness. It is entirely between you and God. No one can stop you from praying. No one can influence God against you. No one can prevent Him from answering your prayers. No one can stop the unfoldment of spiritual understanding. No one can keep from you the good you have demonstrated, or reverse the spiritual blessings God gives you. If you have realized a better understanding of health and harmony, this understanding must unfold outwardly in increased good in your human experience.

Throughout the unfoldment of God's divine plan, reading and studying Christian Science is essential. This is especially true of Mrs. Eddy's works. Many statements set forth in her books seem in the beginning to be incomprehensible. But as you pass through the various phases, they become the key to understanding the allness of God and the unreality of evil. They uncover the animal magnetism that must be handled, and they unfold the truth that destroys it.

The treatment is also absolutely essential. A good treatment heals the claims of animal magnetism. As you experience healing results from your own metaphysical work, your appreciation of what Mrs. Eddy has given humanity knows no bounds. Indeed, it would be extremely difficult, if not impossible, to demonstrate your way through these phases without knowing how to deny the animal magnetism entrenched within, and how to cast it out through affirmations of truth. For this reason, you need to learn this first phase before you graduate to the more advanced phases.

Once you realize the healing power of study and prayer, you should begin relying on your own metaphysical work to heal claims of sickness, lack, discord, etc. You learn to do effective treatments by working to overcome your own problems. As you lay aside your preoccupation with the mortal, material world and go deeper into spiritual things, this consecrated work brings to the surface of your consciousness forms of animal magnetism so buried within that you aren't aware of them. It frees you of them, and brings about more unfoldment of good than you could ever outline or accomplish through human effort alone.

Handling Specific Claims

By making time and space within for God's thoughts to unfold, an understanding of Christian Science begins to take form, and this prepares you to do your own healing work.

Your metaphysical work will be most effective if you work to meet specific claims. Applying treatment to clearly defined problems and needs might be compared to practicing a profession, such as accounting. One can learn the principles of accounting, but then he needs to apply this education to actually keeping books, if he is to become an accredited accountant.

Even so, the concept of treatment must be brought to bear on problems, and the metaphysical work must result in healing. Staying in the absolute and simply "knowing the truth" is not totally effective in de-mesmerizing consciousness. You should learn to use the treatment to heal every claim of animal magnetism as it comes to you to be healed.

There are obvious forms of error that we willingly handle — illness, lack, discordant relationships, experiences that cause us pain, suffering, emotional distress and turmoil. As you first begin a consecrated study of Christian Science, you will most likely treat those problem that cause you the most suffering — problems that obviously need healing.

This healing work should be a stepping-stone to higher demonstrations. An occasional healing leaves untouched the basic mortal elements of the human disposition. Stagnation in Christian Science comes when we only handle error that is causing us to suffer. Such work leaves the rest of the error within uncorrected. Inner reformation should be an on-going effort. If you do not do this work willingly, you are eventually forced into it through the suffering caused by the accumulation of unhandled mortal beliefs and traits.

However, as you progress, you also learn to detect and handle animal magnetism within which is not yet causing you to suffer. This is especially true of those beliefs and traits that seem to be a normal part of your disposition. The warfare with animal magnetism involves healing the entire inner self — not merely the forms of error that cause you to suffer. In your treatment, you must analyze and treat the whole of mortal mind.

Most material beliefs and mortal emotions are universally accepted as a normal part of human disposition. There are many false traits within that seem so natural that most of us never think to challenge them as animal magnetism — self-will, fear, hatred, self-love, self-justification, to name a few. We think in them effortlessly. When we work in the absolute or give a general treatment, this is not enough to bring these errors to light and destroy them. Nor do mortal traits and beliefs fade away with the passing of time. If they go uncorrected, they increase their hold on consciousness until we are forced to correct them through the suffering they cause.

To handle specific claims, the footsteps of treatment must be applied to each claim. Through your metaphysical work, you can define mortal elements seemingly entrenched in the inner self, and then eliminate them by treating yourself for each one. Handle specific forms of error as they are uncovered in your metaphysical work, and you will begin to spiritualize the whole of consciousness,

We are freed of the suffering caused by animal magnetism only by treating each error specifically and ruling it out of our consciousness. There must be a concerted effort to make this happen, and the time to do this is before the belief within develops to the place where it brings on suffering, pain and mental darkness.

Christian Science makes it possible to do this. It clearly separates good and evil, truth and error, the mortal and the immortal, so that you can discern between the claims of animal magnetism and man's real nature in God's likeness. You can then deny specific false claims, and affirm the spiritual facts of being, until the false traits and beliefs give way. Through this work, consciousness is always in a state of gentle chemicalization as false beliefs gradually pass away, and the truth of being unfolds. As specific claims, one by one, surface and disappear, spiritual ideas and qualities unfold to replace them, transforming your mind. Your true identity comes to light, and you find your oneness with God.

SECOND PHASE: DEMONSTRATING THE LAW OF LOVE

The second phase deepens and expands on the healing of specific claims. It focuses on understanding and obeying the law of Love.

When your prayerful work makes the truth active in consciousness, it begins to neutralize the error within. The mind is never so darkened that the Christ-consciousness cannot penetrate it, nor is the mind so hardened that it cannot change.

In the first phase, you begin to treat specific claims that are in need of healing — even traits and beliefs that are considered to be normal. But too often such healings leave unchanged most of our mortal personality. The next spiritual lesson is to learn the meaning of the law of Love and how to obey it. The goal in the second phase is to begin freeing consciousness of mortal traits that violate this law, and to replace them with qualities that reflect the divine Principle, Love.

Over the centuries, many learned men have struggled with the mystery of Godliness. They have tried to enter the spiritual realm through intellectualism and rationalization, philosophies and human interpretations of the Scriptures. It would seem that they were trying to enter heaven on their own terms, without conforming to the law of Love.

Yet Christ Jesus gave the first key to knowing God in his Sermon on the Mount, when he taught his followers to love their enemies. He said. "Bless those that curse you, do good to them that hate you, and pray for them which despitefully use you, and persecute you; that you may be the children of your Father which is in heaven." When a lawyer asked him, "Master, which is the greatest commandment in the law?" Jesus answered him, "Thou shalt love the Lord thy God with all thy heart, and with all thy soul, and with all thy mind. This the first and great commandment. The second is like unto it, Thou shalt love thy neighbor as thyself"

It was John who wrote, "Beloved, let us love one another: for love is of God; and every one that loveth is born of God, and knoweth God . . . God is love; and he that dwelleth in love dwelleth in God, and God in him."

Throughout her writings, Mrs. Eddy refers to the *divine* Principle, Love. She writes in *Science and Health,* "'God is Love.' More than this we cannot ask, higher we cannot look, farther we cannot go." She also states, "Divine Love is infinite. Therefore all that really exists is in and of God, and manifests His love."

Why is spiritual love so important? We live love in obedience to God. It is the great fundamental teaching of Christianity which brings inspiration and healing. It is certainly essential in order to have a better world. But there is a more scientific reason why we must learn to love, one that is basic to the divine plan.

Emergence from the dark, limiting, suffering mortal dream takes place subjectively. It is experienced solely within each individual sphere of thought. *It depends entirely upon the unfoldment of spiritual ideas, or "God's thoughts passing to man," to your consciousness.* This inspiration and enlightenment is absolutely essential to spiritualizing consciousness. It is the silent influence of Truth and Love reaching you from within and transform-

25

ing the inner self. In order for you to experience this unfoldment of ideas, *God must be able to reach you.*

When consciousness is filled with spiritual love, it embodies the qualities of compassion, gentleness, patience, kindness, forgiveness, faith and humility. This soft, gentle, unresisting state of mind is receptive to God's ideas, and so when we pray, the mind is open to receive God's thoughts, and then He can unfold spiritual ideas to you.

But when consciousness is filled with mortal emotions that harden the inner self, when it embodies hate, fear, and self-will, these emotions block out the unfoldment of spiritual ideas. The animal magnetism within prevents the unfoldment of spiritual enlightenment and inspiration which would mean its destruction, and so God cannot reach you. A mentality hardened by anger, self-love, irritation, impatience, self-righteousness, envy, jealousy, stubbornness, fear, is never receptive to God's thoughts. It cannot understand the kingdom of God — the atmosphere of Love, divinely tender, patient, warm, gentle, and pure.

In order for a progressive understanding of God to unfold, the inner self must have a mental atmosphere that can relate to the thoughts of divine Love. The purpose of your metaphysical work is to allow God to mold and remold the inner self until you "awake in His likeness." *A mind softened by spiritual love is flexible and yielding to God's thoughts, and so it can be transformed through the spiritual ideas that God gives to it. A mind hardened by animal magnetism rejects and rebels against the divine influence, and so God cannot reach it.*

Christian Science reveals the difference between the mortal traits that harden the mind and the spiritual qualities that soften it. The mortal elements that shut out spiritual unfoldment are not necessarily classified by the average mind as wrong or sinful, mainly because they are so universal. These false traits are so intermingled with the qualities of human goodness, that it is difficult to separate the two. They are so common we never question them or consider giving them up. As a rule, we practice them daily. We may even justify and cling to them as our personality. Even when we know they are wrong, this does not necessarily rid us of them. We go on violating the law of Love out of habit; and in so doing, we remain in the darkness of animal magnetism's influence.

It is likely that we consider ourselves to be good and loving, but sensual and personal emotions are not the same as spiritual love. They are based on personal sense and are the mortal traits and emotions within that harden the mind. Unless the mind is permeated with spiritual love, it continues to embody ungodlike elements which are opaque, rocklike, dense and unyielding. These subtle forms of animal magnetism cause the mind to be inflexible, preventing us from finding our inner rapport with God. The more pronounced the mortal traits, the more hardened the mind is to the healing touch of the Christ. When the mind is rigidly set in negative thought-habits, a very suffering experience is usually the only thing that will change it. Even though we study Christian Science and understand how to give a treatment, mortal traits still remain embedded in consciousness, to be uncovered and overcome.

As we uncover these traits and beliefs, and do specific work to overcome them, we gradually rise above them. By recognizing them as animal magnetism and not as a permanent part of our real selfhood, we can be free of them. However, we cannot overcome them through human effort alone. We transform the inner self when we think deeply about the law of Love, and through daily study and prayer, replace false traits with qualities that reflect divine Love.

This is a simple requirement — to demonstrate spiritual love. Yet it seems extremely difficult to do — to be love, to think love, to live love. Why aren't we more into love? Perhaps because we shut out spiritual love when we mistake the negative, sensual, material emotions for this love of God. Yet we must learn to love, for spiritual love is the secret to finding our oneness with God. Through love, we enter the secret place that is hidden from minds hardened by animal magnetism.

Comparing the Three Degrees in "Science and Health"

The second phase, demonstrating the law of Love, begins the more advanced practice of Christian Science. It teaches us to go beneath the surface of the mind and analyze the innermost thoughts and emotions, to compare them to spiritual love, and through study and prayer to free the mind of them.

We find a guideline for this purification of thought on page 115 of *Science and Health.* We have here the scientific translation of both mortal mind and immortal Mind:

SCIENTIFIC TRANSLATION OF IMMORTAL MIND

GOD: Divine Principle, Life, Truth, Love, Soul, Spirit, Mind.
       (Marginal heading: Divine Synonyms)
MAN: God's spiritual idea, individual, perfect, eternal.
       (Marginal heading: Divine Image)
IDEA: An image of Mind; the immediate object of under-
standing. - *Webster.*
       (Marginal heading: Divine reflection)

SCIENTIFIC TRANSLATION OF MORTAL MIND

First Degree: Depravity.
PHYSICAL. Evil beliefs, passions and appetites, fear, depraved will, self-justification, pride, envy, deceit, hatred,
revenge, sin, sickness, disease, death.
       (Marginal heading: Unreality)

Second Degree: Evil beliefs disappearing.
MORAL. Humanity, honesty, affection, compassion, hope,
faith, meekness, temperance.
       (Marginal heading: Transitional Qualities)

Third Degree: Understanding.
SPIRITUAL. Wisdom, purity, spiritual understanding, spiri-
tual power, love, health, holiness.
(Marginal heading: Reality)

We see that the First and Second Degrees of "The Scientific Translation of Mortal Mind" are concerned with emotions. The
cold, hard, selfish emotions of the First Degree dissolve and fade
out as we emerge into the soft, warm, unselfed love of the Second
Degree. In *Science and Health,* Mrs. Eddy writes of this transformation, "In patient obedience to a patient God, let us labor to
dissolve with the universal solvent of Love the adamant of error, —
self-will, self-justification, and self-love, — which wars against spirituality and is the law of sin and death."

Let us consider carefully the difference between the First
and Second Degrees. The First Degree defines animal magnetism:
"Evil beliefs, passions and appetites, fear, depraved will, self-justification, pride, envy, deceit, hatred, revenge, sin, sickness, disease,
death." I'm sure we must congratulate ourselves that we are not in
that Degree — but how can we be so sure?

Carefully compare the First Degree with the Second
Degree: "Humanity, honesty, affection, compassion, hope, faith,
meekness, temperance." Think carefully about these warm, gentle,
Godlike qualities. The Second Degree stems almost entirely from
the synonym Love. The qualities of the Second Degree precede
the Third Degree. Therefore, in order to reach the Third Degree,
we cannot pass over the Second Degree, or go around it, or come
back to it later. We reach the Third Degree by passing *through* the
Second Degree. We must demonstrate spiritual love before we can
graduate to "wisdom, purity, spiritual understanding, spiritual power,
love, health, holiness."

We should not assume that we are already in the Second
Degree, moving into the Third, until we have thoroughly analyzed

the First and Second Degree, for it is likely that we unknowingly manifest so many subtle elements in the First Degree that we have not yet entered the Second Degree to any great extent. The First Degree covers many forms of sin so commonly accepted and practiced that we never consider them to be wrong.

There is hatred, for example. Hatred includes animosity, hostility, antagonism, resentment, irritation, impatience, anger, temper. How can spiritual ideas enter a mind secretly or openly raging with others, malpracticing on them, emitting what amounts to a mental poison towards those it hates. We think we do not hate, but every thought or emotion that is not kind, gentle, patient, affectionate, forgiving, tolerant, compassionate, and understanding, is related to hatred.

Hatred includes being unforgiving. When hateful things are done to us that we do not deserve, how often do we react with 'justified' hatred. Do we feel we cannot forgive those who have ignorantly or intentionally wronged us? Are we secretly bitter, cynical, resentful, revengeful towards others? This is one of the most hardened states of mind imaginable, and it is a very common one. Until we learn to forgive and forget, God has a difficult time reaching us.

Consider criticism. Criticism is a form of hatred. We must take care about being critical, for how can we hold criticism and compassion in the same mind at the same time? Criticism includes disapproval, rejection of another, self-righteousness. It means being opinionated, judgmental, cold and hard-hearted. It is void of spiritual love and shuts out the Christ.

This one example alone shows how common are the emotions of the First Degree. They are everywhere. Anyone who thinks critical, judgmental thoughts of another is in the First Degree.

The same is true of those who are opinionated, proud, stubborn, self-willed. Personal sense is always arguing for and justifying its opinions and prejudices. There is no meekness or kindness in an egotistical mentality. Those who argue with others, will also argue with God. Their mind is so rebellious that God cannot lead them out of mortal mind.

We need to give much consideration to self-will — especially that form of depraved will that will not be crossed, thwarted, or denied. This is a mental condition so opaque as to be void of Christlike love. It is insensitive, self-righteous, unforgiving, demanding, angry, vindictive. It is so lacking affection and compassion that it cannot hear the "still, small voice."

There are other mortal traits in the First Degree that are accepted as normal, even desirable. To name a few, we can be a perfectionist. We can use others deceitfully. We can dominate others with self-righteousness, claiming that we know what is best for them. We can interfere with the lives of others or manipulate them. We can seek revenge or find a scapegoat when things go wrong. We can be proud of our human goodness. We can be so preoccupied with the cares and troubles of the world that we have no time for God. We can be mesmerized by pride of intellect, background, education, or accomplishment. We can look down on others as beneath us, thus excluding and rejecting them. We may even be lovingly self-righteous, lovingly dominating, lovingly opinionated, or silently disapproving, angry, cold, resentful. Some people are so obsessed with the misery, dishonesty, crime and corruption in the world that they are blind to the universe of God's creating. This habit of magnifying evil is practically the same as saying there is no God. If we deny God, good, and insist on the reality of evil, then God cannot find any receptivity in thought through which to show us the kingdom of heaven within.

This list of mortal traits is an example of the forms of animal magnetism that are found in the First Degree. The human mind is tightly closed to spiritual enlightenment if it is darkened by too many of these emotions.

When we study the qualities found in the Second Degree, we find mainly emotions that are expressions of unselfed love: humility, patience, forbearance, understanding, compatibility, affec-

31

tion, tenderness, gentleness, kindness, forgiveness, graciousness, warmth, generosity, thoughtfulness, sensitivity, tact, charity, virtue, purity, goodness, mercy, tolerance, decency, faithfulness, integrity, moral strength, fairness, justice, truthfulness, sincerity, reliability, steadfastness, stability, self-control, gratitude, tranquility, and peace. A mind filled with these qualities is receptive to God's thoughts.

We must go *through* the Second Degree and demonstrate spiritual love before we can enter the Third Degree. Each Degree is so clearly defined that we can leave the First Degree and demonstrate the Second, because we now know the difference between the two, and we have the Science which makes the transition from one to the other possible.

Analyzing Our Thoughts and Emotions

It is best not to assume that we have outgrown the First Degree until we have made a thorough analysis of our inner thoughts and emotions. It has been my experience that year after year, as I pursue this work, hidden forms of self-will, fear and other negative emotions surface from the subconscious mind. The treatment loosens them and brings them to light to pass away. Our demonstration of the traits found in the First Degree continues indefinitely, as we pass through one phase after another in the divine plan.

If inner change seems difficult to achieve, it is because you are trying to demonstrate spiritual qualities that are new and unknown to you. Have you ever experienced a state of mind void of hate and filled with spiritual love, or one free of fear and filled with trust in God? The mental state of the Second Degree is so different from your present disposition that it requires a great deal of study and prayer to work out of one into the other. As you undertake this work, always remember that God will unfold the inspiration and enlightenment that brings forth this higher state of mind if you seek it humbly, earnestly, persistently.

Through learning to obey the law of Love, you overcome the animal magnetism in consciousness which is the underlying cause of sickness, disease, age, discord and limitation. You heal false traits in consciousness that tend to become recurring, chronic, incurable beliefs of sickness, disease, age and so on. Physical problems caused by mortal emotions disappear, for they are the effects of mortal traits and beliefs. In demonstrating the Second Degree, you take control of your emotions, and mellow or mature into quiet thoughts of caring, affection, forgiveness, gentleness, humility, patience, and gratitude. These result in a mental atmosphere that is pliable, soft, receptive, filled with hope and faith — an atmosphere that is open to revelation and easily influenced by God.

There is a universal claim that human nature is almost impossible to change. But Christian Science makes it possible to completely transform the inner self. When you know the difference between the Three Degrees, and can handle animal magnetism in the treatment, you can bring about such spiritualization of thought that your entire disposition is transformed.

In *Science and Health,* we read of the need to examine our thinking, "Anatomy, when conceived of spiritually, is mental self-knowledge, and consists in the dissection of thoughts to discover their quality, quantity, and origin. Are thoughts divine or human? That is the important question. This branch of study is indispensable to the excision of error. The anatomy of Christian Science teaches when and how to probe the self-inflicted wounds of selfishness, malice, envy, and hate. It teaches the control of mad ambition. It unfolds the hallowed influences of unselfishness, philanthropy, spiritual love."

Living Spiritual Love

The question is, How do you live spiritual love? When you think of love, are you more concerned with being loved, than in giving love? Demonstrating spiritual love means reflecting God's love, loving others before they love you, giving them approval, kindness, thoughtfulness, understanding, patience, forgiving their differences with you, not taking offense at what they say or do, not being disappointed when they do not live up to your expectations.

Spiritual love which softens consciousness and enables you to commune with God, cannot be superficial or hypocritical. You cannot appear to be loving while you go on secretly harboring criticism, envy, vindictiveness, resentment, fear, or hatred. Your work is to detect negative thoughts and feelings hidden deep within and replace them with spiritual love until you do not think or feel them any longer. You need to have loving thoughts of others, especially when you are alone. You need to dwell in loving thoughts all the time. It takes tremendous self-discipline never to think critical, hateful, angry, hurtful, unforgiving, revengeful thoughts *secretly*; but this is the real requirement of the Second Degree. You can do this as you face the traits of the First Degree that seem to control you and refuse to be handled by them any longer.

There seems to be in human nature a host of false traits over which we believe we have little or no control. Does fear ever handle you and you cannot get beyond it? Does anger, depression, hurt feelings, or hatred well up and control you, and you cannot put it out? It is evident that the human mind alone cannot overcome false emotions through its own will-power. But you can overcome them when your treatment is focused on specific emotions. You can treat such emotions through affirmation and denial, just as you would treat a physical claim. Specific work is required to impersonalize these forms of sin and destroy them. A long and determined effort to overcome ingrained thought-habits and emotions may be needed; but if you persist, you can be free of them.

This is possible because false traits and beliefs are not a permanent part of your being. Beyond and above mortal mind, your immortal selfhood remains forever safe in God. Therefore, you can overcome mortal traits that claim to separate you from Him. As you focus on uncovering and correcting the animal magnetism within, the truth, active in consciousness, begins to penetrate the dark cloud of mortal mind, and to heal the emotions through which animal magnetism seems to control you. A softening of the inner self takes place.

Such metaphysical work is greatly helped by the study of the synonym Love. Then through the treatment, handle animal magnetism coming in the form of negative thoughts and emotions. By facing down negative emotions and denying their reality, you force them to give out. You can feel them dissolve within, and in the mental space that they had occupied there unfolds the spiritual qualities of your true selfhood in God's likeness. The mind is never so hardened that it cannot change. Therefore you can specifically handle false traits one by one, and rise above them.

As you persist in demonstrating the law of Love, your disposition begins to change. The hardened mental state of the First Degree softens. The rigid mentality becomes flexible and receptive to new ideas. The law of Love becomes normal to you, and you live it effortlessly. You have the strength, wisdom, and courage to be loving, and your love is consistently patient, kind, forgiving to everyone everywhere all the time.

It is not easy to demonstrate the Second Degree. It takes incredible strength to be loving to those who are unloving, kind to those who are unkind, forgiving with the unforgiving, generous when there is no reciprocation — or even an acknowledgment of your generosity. It takes enormous self-discipline to leave unsaid sharp, hurtful, angry, critical words when others use them on you. It takes great dedication to discipline yourself never *to think unloving thoughts when you are alone.*

Most likely you are aware of mortal traits within that need correcting. You will find, as you progress in Christian Science, that you are constantly sifting your feelings and motives to uncover the error hidden in the inmost thoughts. Through daily treatment, you can affirm the truth about yourself. You can argue for the fact that you do express compassion, kindness, gentleness, patience, forgiveness, unselfed love, for these are the qualities of your true selfhood. They are already established as your God-given nature.

Then you can turn on animal magnetism and vehemently deny that it can mesmerize you into expressing the negative emotions and beliefs of a false selfhood. Realize that these false traits are mortal beliefs, and they have no more power than you give them. Deny them. Refuse to entertain them, for they violate the law of Love.

Such treatment has to be repeated again and again in order to free consciousness of certain false traits, but as these traits give out, you find yourself unable to act or react in an unloving way towards others. You don't *want* to criticize or judge them. You don't *want* to be angry or impatient with them. You don't *want* to hurt them. You don't *want* to criticize them. You are able to forgive them when they do not do what you expect of them. Then you are actually living the law of Love.

As you leave the First Degree and move into the Second, the Christ-consciousness rules out the anti-Christ. Love softens the inner self and makes it receptive to God's thoughts. God teaches you from within, for nothing can shut out His thoughts except your own violation of the law of Love.

As you demonstrate and live in an atmosphere of gentle stillness and quiet humility, you feel close to God and are sensitive to His presence. Moments of revelation add up to significant mental changes and impressive healings. At some point in your demonstration of the Second Degree, you are strong enough to begin the third phase.

THIRD PHASE: DESTROYING THE ILLUSION OF MATTER

In *Science and Health,* Mrs. Eddy writes, "Spirit and its formations are the only realities of being. Matter disappears under the microscope of Spirit." She also tells us, "Matter, examined in the light of divine metaphysics, disappears." The unreality of matter must be understood and proven in Christian Science. The third phase begins this demonstration.

As you learn to live the law of Love, you come to realize that spiritual love alone does not usher you into the kingdom of God, for problems remain that do not yield to your metaphysical work. Evil continues to seem very real, very ominous, and the illusion of matter remains a concrete conviction. Human goodness and spiritual love, however strong and pure, do not always protect you from the harmful effects of the belief in matter and its laws. Even though you may have great faith in all that Christian Science teaches, and know how to give a healing treatment, and are making a better demonstration of spiritual love, the belief in the reality and power of evil and matter continue to be present in the heart of consciousness; the illusion of matter still produces sickness, discord, and limitation; the solid conviction of a mortal life in a material universe, imprisoned in a physical body, has not changed.

At this point, you need to go deeper into Christian Science and challenge the belief in the illusion of matter. Many mortal conditions and physical claims, caused by an entrenched belief in matter, will not heal until you begin to see that matter is mesmeric illusion. Therefore you cannot stagnate in the second phase. You have to press on into the third phase and begin this demonstration.

In the orderly process of the divine plan, this is the next major breakthrough. Yet how often do Christian Scientists consider overcoming the belief in matter? We may handle it superficially in meeting a physical claim, and we may theoretically accept Mrs. Eddy's statements regarding the unreality of matter; but somewhere in time everyone will have to handle the entire belief in matter and outgrow this dark, ignorant illusion.

Have you ever considered challenging your belief in matter? Have you ever seriously asked the question, How can it be that there is no matter? And if so, did you expect God to answer it?

Perhaps you feel this is too much to expect of your present demonstration of Christian Science, but you cannot begin too soon the work of seeing through the mist of matter, In so doing, God is preparing you to understand the answer, and then He will reveal the answer to you.

Matter a Veil over the Mind

Although matter seems to be a dense, hard, opaque substance outside of consciousness, it is in reality hypnotic illusion, a veil cast over the mind, blinding you to the spiritual universe and the man of God's creating. Resolving the illusion of matter is entirely a subjective experience.

Matter seems to exist objectively, constructing a world outside of consciousness which appears to be concrete reality. We seem to be small entities coping with universal laws of material cause and effect. When we think of being free of matter and its laws, we usually see this as coming through death, or after death, or as being off in some distant time and place. But in fact, somewhere in time, we must pray our way out of this illusion. And we can begin doing so right now. The sooner we begin, the sooner we will be free of the illusion.

Since matter is a subjective illusion, the dissolving of the belief in matter comes about subjectively. And this begins when we have demonstrated the second phase sufficiently to be prepared for this revelation. There are several reasons why we must pass through the second phase before we can face and overcome the belief in matter.

First, overcoming the belief in matter is a holy event. It is a revelation that appears in a mental atmosphere that is softened by the Second Degree and is receptive to new ideas. There must be a yearning to understand the unreality of matter, and an absolute faith that Mrs. Eddy's teachings on matter's unreality are correct, even though the senses tell us otherwise. We must be flexible enough to accept and adapt to a vision that is so radical that it gives us a completely different view of creation and ourselves.

Second, the real universe is one of divine Love. The substance of creation is not hard, dense, opaque matter. It is not governed by ominous, threatening, cruel, cold, mindless material laws.

It is a warm, harmless, benign, good, safe creation governed by the laws of divine Love. In the hardened state of the First Degree, there is nothing within consciousness to relate to a universe that is an atmosphere of pure love — a universe governed by God's will, rather than mindless material forces. Only a mental atmosphere filled with spiritual love can understand and accept God's answer to the question of matter's unreality. Therefore, in order to understand the unreality of matter, thought must embody strong qualities of love and be compatible with a spiritual universe created and governed by the divine Principle, Love. To discern God as the underlying cause of all things, we need to reflect His love. Therefore phase two must precede the dissolving of the illusion of matter.

Having learned the law of Love to some extent, and now questioning God as to the unreality of matter, you can work metaphysically to prepare for this mental breakthrough. Prayerful study of all that Mrs. Eddy writes on matter and related subjects, combined with the treatment, is fundamental to this third phase.

Proving the Unreality of Matter

In *Unity of Good,* Mrs. Eddy tells us, "With Christ, Life was not merely a sense of existence, but a sense of might and ability to subdue material conditions." In the third phase of this work, you undertake the challenge of demonstrating this same dominion. You think and pray your way out of the illusion of matter. Without this effort, you may accept theoretically the statement that matter is unreal, but you continue believing in it as a reality, because it is all you have ever known. Matter is more real to you than God.

To be free of the illusion of matter, you begin by assuming the responsibility for overcoming it. Time does not dissolve the belief in it. General work in Christian Science does not break it down. A demonstration of spiritual love in the second phase does not do it. You dis-abuse your mind of this belief only when you take the initiative and do specific metaphysical work to break the claim that matter is real. This is one of the most important demonstrations you will ever make.

Before physicists of this century discovered the nonmaterial nature of the universe, Mrs. Eddy wrote in *Science and Health,* "Divine metaphysics explains away matter." She also wrote, "There is no life, truth, intelligence nor substance in matter. All is infinite Mind and its infinite manifestation, for God is All-in-all." She did not teach mind over matter. She said *there is no matter.*

Today physicists also are saying that there is no matter in terms of a hard, solid mass. Although the nonmaterial nature of the universe has become an accepted fact, the human mind remains trapped in the *belief* that matter is real, because the human mind, without an understanding of Christian Science, has nothing to put in the place of the illusion of matter. Human consciousness cannot de-mesmerize itself and transcend its own material beliefs without Christian Science, and so this opaque illusion of matter remains. As long as the illusion continues, so does the suffering it produces.

Two Viewpoints

We study Christian Science to understand God, and to escape the suffering and limitations imposed by the belief in matter and mortality. But in so doing, we find two conflicting viewpoints of man and the universe emerging.

Mrs. Eddy says there is no matter, and yet we believe we live in a material universe and a material body. In fact, matter seems more real and powerful than God. Yet Christ Jesus, John, and, two thousand years later, Mrs. Eddy, all had a great vision that revealed to them the spiritual nature of man and the universe. As we progress spiritually, we come to experience the same revelation.

The universe occupies a large part of our thinking. If we are going to know our oneness with God, we must spiritualize our concept of His universe. We cannot be spiritual man while holding in consciousness a material universe. We need to discern the whole of creation in its spiritual perfection — both man and the universe. To experience this revelation is a unique event that transforms our image of creation.

Once this mental breakthrough takes place, we no longer believe matter is unreal. We *know* it is unreal, and so we begin to demonstrate dominion over it. Before Christian Science is introduced into consciousness, we have one viewpoint of the universe and man — the material viewpoint. All things seem to be created and sustained by the forces of matter. We believe atomic form and energy to be controlled by the mindless forces of gravity, chemistry, electro-magnetism, nuclear forces, and so on. These forces appear to act regardless of the suffering and discord that they inflict on living things. They exclude a thinking cause. When we embrace this material view as solid conviction, matter seems real. Our image of the universe is dense, dark, heavy, opaque. We appear at the mercy of godless forces and laws. When the mind is hardened with self-will, fear, hatred, etc., it views creation through a mortal mind, and sees its own erring state of mind objectified in a material universe and man.

The image of a creation formed and controlled by mindless matter is hypnotic illusion, which originates in animal magnetism, and attributes everything to physical causes. It is a state of mind which continues to mesmerize us until we begin to challenge it in Christian Science.

Christian Science introduces a different and opposing viewpoint, showing man and the universe to be spiritual, not material. Furthermore, this Science specifically defines the structure, qualities, laws, and energies that create and govern the universe, and attributes all cause and effect to God.

Mrs. Eddy does not say there are two universes — one material and one spiritual. She says there are two viewpoints of the same universe — the false, material one and the true, spiritual one. Christian Science then accurately defines the false material illusion and the real spiritual creation. The spiritual view presents the true image of the universe created and governed by the one Mind, God — an unseen spiritual cause that is loving, good, wise, intelligent, harmonious, and perfect.

As Christian Science unfolds to consciousness a second view of creation, a spiritual view, we have two conflicting views — both seeming real and logical. At this point, although we may believe the spiritual view is the right one, the material view remains the one that is real to us. It is the one we are used to. The spiritual universe and man seem vague, theoretical, almost impossible to understand.

Although we are aware of two views, usually this dualism in consciousness remains unchanged and we do not progress beyond it, because the belief in matter is never specifically handled and broken down. Before we learn to work in the treatment, overcoming this illusion seems beyond our present ability to succeed in such a seemingly impossible goal.

But now, with the textbook to study, and an understanding of the treatment, we can challenge the belief in matter — specifically challenge it — and keep at it until the mesmerism thins out, and we see through the mist of matter.

The Fourth Dimension of Spirit

How do we see through the illusion of matter? Actually, it is very simple. *We add a spiritual dimension to the universe.* Mrs. Eddy wrote that there is no matter because she, like John and the Master Christian, saw through the three dimensional universe and discerned underlying it the fourth dimension of Spirit, God. She wrote in *Miscellaneous Writings,* "Christian Science translates Mind, God, to mortals. It is the infinite calculus defining the line, plane, space, and fourth dimension of Spirit."

We begin to overcome matter by visualizing an additional dimension to the universe. This dimension is not something we are creating and putting into the universe. It is already here. It has *always* been here. It fills the eternal now. We are presently in the spiritual universe, but we are blinded to this fact by the veil of matter cast over consciousness. *This mental blindness is wholly subjective, and the light which destroys this darkness also appears subjectively.* Christian Science gives us this light, this understanding, which spiritualizes and transforms our image of creation and man. In doing so, the substance of Spirit appears where the material universe seems to be. We are merely overcoming our ignorance of the spiritual dimension and our insensitivity to it. Through Christian Science, we learn of the true structure and nature of this unseen realm.

Although matter seems real, it is nothing more than an erroneous state of mind, a solid conviction that continues to mesmerize us until we press through the edges of the mind and add another dimension to all things. This "fourth dimension of Spirit" is the intelligence and love governing all atomic structure and behavior. We read in *Miscellaneous Writings,* "Atomic action is Mind, not matter. It is neither the energy of matter, the result of organization, nor the outcome of life infused into matter: it is infinite Spirit, Truth, Life defiant of error or matter." To the degree that we understand this, matter disappears.

The Spiritual Age

To help us visualize this emerging of a fourth dimension, let us approach it as the foundation of a new age — a spiritual age. This new age is comparable to the dawning of the scientific age. If we were to go back three hundred years, we would find a world totally ignorant or unconscious of a scientific dimension in the universe. Everyone, even those who could vaguely foresee the coming of a scientific age, had a very limited vision of the future. Their ignorance did not change the fact that a universal scientific dimension was a reality — a concrete reality that had always existed. Try to imagine a world ignorant of the scientific dimension compared to our world today totally submerged in scientific technology. You can see how this dimension has gradually come to light and transformed civilization.

Now, what does Christian Science tell us? It says that there exists yet another dimension to the universe. We are, at this time, as uneducated in the nature of this spiritual dimension as the people of medieval times were regarding the scientific dimension. Yet this Godlike dimension exists as a concrete reality — as real as the scientific dimension. It is destined to shape the spiritual age as surely as the scientific dimension was destined to shape the scientific age.

Therefore, in challenging the illusion of matter, we are exploring this new dimension as pioneers in the spiritual age. We are destroying the veil of matter that seems to separate us from God. And this is done subjectively. Matter is nothing but the seeming absence of divine intelligence — the absence of an understanding of the spiritual realm.

Spiritual Translation of the Universe

Because the seeming reality of matter is so strongly established in consciousness, it would seem that if we wiped out matter, we would destroy the entire universe. Actually it is just the opposite. When matter and material cause and effect begin to fade out, spiritual substance, cause and effect replace them. Our metaphysical work does not produce a vacuum in consciousness. We simply expand upon our mental image of creation by adding to it another dimension — a fourth dimension of divine intelligence and love, creating and controlling all things. Christian Science is the *only* metaphysical system which accurately reveals the nature of this hidden realm.

I recall vividly the first time I glimpsed the fourth dimension of Spirit. I had been struggling for several years to resolve this duality of the material and the spiritual viewpoints. I asked God constantly how it could be that there was no matter. I studied all that Mrs. Eddy had written on the subject. I also read a number of books on present day physics, which were very helpful in visualizing the non-material nature of creation. But still matter seemed a very hard, dense, solid reality.

Then one night I was standing at the window looking out at the moon, pondering this mystery of matter's unreality. At first the moon appeared to be a hard, rocklike thing, held in place by the mindless force of gravity. It was a cold, heavy, opaque form of mindless matter. Then suddenly it became transparent. I saw that every atom that made up the moon was created and controlled by the thought-forces of Mind. The moon was a creation of Love, held in place by the power of God, not by a mindless field of gravity. The moon became weightless, nonmaterial. It was a spiritual idea that belonged wholly to the one Mind.

For a short time, matter completely disappeared, and I was conscious only of spiritual reality. Yet the object I was seeing did not change physically. It did not need to change, for it was already an idea in the spiritual universe. But my mental image of it changed. I saw it complete in its spiritual dimension. In *Science and Health,* Mrs. Eddy tells us, "Thought will finally be understood and seen in all form, substance, and color; but without material accompaniments . . . God is His own infinite Mind, and expresses all."

My first vision into the spiritual dimension was limited to my view of the moon. But at that moment, all duality disappeared. I had only the single viewpoint, and I knew I had an answer as to the unreality of matter. Gradually I have been able to expand upon this vision to include all things to a small degree. I am continuing to work out of the belief in matter, but I know now how to do it.

I share my experience with you so you will know what to expect. I am sure each of us will experience this revelation in an individual way. Your revelation may first involve a single object, as mine did, or it may gradually permeate all that you are conscious of, or it may suddenly fill the universe, as in Mrs. Eddy's vision. In this experience, nothing outwardly changes. Everything is still there with forms distinctly defined, physically the same. The change comes in the mental atmosphere within. What is believed to be mindless matter becomes the spiritual substance of the universe. The true cause underlying the universe is revealed to be a loving, benign, intelligent one. When we discern God, Spirit, as the only cause, everything takes on a new dimension, and matter disappears.

I cannot emphasize enough the spiritualizing effect on consciousness that this revelation brings about. You think your way out of matter into Spirit, and this revelation brings your first real breakthrough into spiritual reality. It takes place within your own consciousness. It is totally subjective — a change in how you think, a very radical change. It takes place through study and prayer, for this vision is a gift from God. He unfolds it to the waiting thought that is prepared to receive it. It transforms the inmost thoughts. Once this mental breakthrough comes, you no longer believe that matter is unreal. You *know* it is unreal, and you begin to demonstrate your dominion over it.

Handling the Belief in Matter

This unfoldment does not come without a great deal of prayerful work. First, you need to recognize that the present view of creation is a false one. Do your surroundings seem dense, hard, heavy, opaque, godless — the product of the mindless forces of matter and its laws? Are they purely physical to you? Then the material view is still the one that seems real to you. But as your study of Christian Science reveals the spiritual nature of creation, you have the material view in conflict with the spiritual view. You will begin to resolve this conflict through the treatment, by denying the material view and affirming the spiritual. You can deny matter and its laws, and affirm God as the one and only cause. You can argue *for* the spiritual view and *against* the material view. You can ask God, patiently and humbly, "How is it that there is no matter?"

You should strive to find the spiritual answer to the conflict in these two viewpoints. Push against the edges of the mind in order to see beyond the material into the spiritual. Visualize a state of consciousness above and beyond the one you now think in. Reach out for it, and wait patiently on God to reveal it to you.

You will not achieve this breakthrough without a great effort to do so. Just as mortal traits do not yield unless you specifically handle each one, neither does the belief in matter yield unless you specifically handle it. If you strive to discern spiritual reality, there comes, sometime and in some way, the initial breakthrough into this spiritual realm.

When this happens, the veil of matter lifts, and you see through the physical universe into the fourth dimension of Spirit. The dense, opaque world of matter begins to dissolve, and all things slowly take on a transparency. Outwardly, they remain the same three dimensional objects they have always been, but they now have underlying them a Godlike cause.

With this revelation, matter begins to fade out of thought. This foretells the time when you will think in the spiritual reality of all things as easily as you now think in the seeming reality of matter.

At first, you may simply glimpse this hidden realm in some small way, but when you do, this is your breakthrough. You know then that there is something more to the universe than material cause and effect. Your study of Christian Science takes on new meaning. You start to develop a single viewpoint of all things — the spiritual viewpoint. You actually begin to think in a deeper, more enlightened state of mind.

The capacity to understand divine reality is in all of us. We develop this capacity through the various phases of the divine plan. As we go through these phases, Christian Science becomes increasingly logical, scientific, meaningful. It gives us an advanced intelligence, and greater dominion over evil. Once this unfoldment of the spiritual dimension comes, it cannot be lost. It continues to expand, and matter slowly fades out until we think naturally, effortlessly in the spiritual viewpoint

The Spiritual Qualities of the Fourth Dimension

With Christian Science, we not only discern the presence of a spiritual realm, but we can define its nature and structure. This is Mrs. Eddy's great gift to the world — she scientifically defined this invisible, intangible dimension. And now, through our own prayerful work, we can define it for ourselves.

Upon entering this fourth dimension, we feel the presence of God filling the universe. We are conscious of the gentleness with which God creates and maintains all things. This thinking cause is the divine Principle, Love, and all that transpires in the universe is in and of Love. There is no force or drive or stress in the activity of Love. All things unfold effortlessly, according to the plan of the one Mind. There are no cruel laws, no harmful effects, no conflicts, no "survival of the fittest." Only the warm, gentle action of God unfolding all things harmoniously in accord with divine law and order.

The powerful presence of Love, the allness of Spirit, the nothingness of matter, is explained again and again throughout Mrs. Eddy's writings. She shows that we do not annihilate the material universe and man. We translate them back into their spiritual state.

When we strive for this spiritual awakening and find it, this great mental breakthrough transforms consciousness. It may first come as a small awakening, a single moment when matter completely vanishes from thought, and we glimpse the divine nature of God's creation. But to see this once, is to realize the spiritual answer to the unreality of matter. From then on, we start to translate all things from matter to Spirit.

As we gain this breakthrough, and establish it as the one viewpoint, we are secure in God's keeping, safely hidden in "the fourth dimension of Spirit."

Because this revelation is totally subjective, no one can discern it for you — but neither can anyone prevent you from finding it. It unfolds in the heart of consciousness, where it should be nurtured secretly, prayerfully, quietly, until it becomes established.

As the vision grows stronger, it brings a lightness and freedom that cannot be described. Many material beliefs drop away because you know there is no matter. Material cause and effect are no longer as real and powerful as before. You begin to see that God is All-in-all, that you are living in the spiritual universe now.

Today, we are entering the spiritual age. The spiritual dimension exists, whether we discern its presence or not. It is a reality that always has been and always will be. In challenging the illusion of matter, we are pioneers, exploring mankind's initial entrance into this new dimension. As this dimension comes to light, it will be understood through divine qualities, and our universe will be seen as a holy place. Matter will pass away like a dark dream, and the spiritual realm will be as concrete and real to us as the scientific dimension is today. Matter will be unknown and humanity will be unified in one viewpoint of creation.

Fourth Phase: Proving the Unreality of Evil

In *Science and Health,* Mrs. Eddy states, "Evil is nothing, no thing, mind, nor power." To a world that seems to be a victim of discord, disease, and death, this absolute statement of evil's nonexistence has often been misunderstood and ridiculed. But recall how she denied the reality of matter in an age submerged in a materialistic philosophy that was universally accepted as scientific truth. In the nineteenth century, matter was seen as hard, impenetrable atoms; in the twentieth century, it is seen as a form of energy with no more substance than a thought or feeling. Indeed, it is now being defined as a state of consciousness, confirming that there is no matter as we think of it. Likewise Mrs. Eddy's statement regarding the unreality of evil will eventually be universally accepted as true.

In the fourth phase, you become part of the *avant garde* in establishing for yourself and all mankind the fact that evil is unreal. Through your own battle with animal magnetism, you prove it to be nothing.

When you understand that evil is nothing, this marks a great turning point in your life. It transforms consciousness. When you challenge the reality of animal magnetism, and carry the battle through to the end, you have a dominion over evil that cannot be gained in any other way. Your healing work becomes quick and powerful, for you control evil; it no longer controls you.

The Individual's Armageddon

The war with animal magnetism could be classified as each individual's Armageddon. You must pass *through* this warfare with evil in order to reach the kingdom within. The previous phases prepare you to undertake this confrontation.

In overcoming false traits and the belief in matter, you have some experience in handling animal magnetism. You have successfully dealt with what could be called the secondary forms, or the *effects* of evil. When you understand the unreality of matter, you have come a long way out of mortal mind — but not far enough. Evil is still operating within consciousness as a seeming power greater than God — a power that produces sickness, disease, mental and emotional suffering, limitation, discord, age and death. Your spiritual advancement to this point does not completely protect you from all beliefs in evil. You need now to handle the cause of mortal mind and matter — *animal magnetism itself.*

As students of Christian Science, we accept on faith the fact that evil is nothing, but deep within, we continue to believe it is real. The belief in its reality remains until we challenge evil, and begin to demonstrate some degree of dominion over it. We need to learn how to face the most aggressive forms of animal magnetism and stand absolutely unintimidated by their seeming reality. When we have no fear of evil, we can face it with the truth and reduce its mesmeric influence to nonexistence.

When we reach the fourth phase of the divine plan, there remains this last great spiritual lesson — learning the nothingness of evil. We must go through this trial, this battle with evil, in order to learn that animal magnetism has no power, no reality. As we do, we lose even more of the mortal traits and beliefs embedded in consciousness, and see more clearly the unreality of matter.

Until we can control evil and destroy it, we should not assume that we understand its nothingness. Sometimes when we have been through severe trials and have survived them, we may think that we understand this point in Christian Science. Certainly, to endure adversity and come through it is commendable. But the purpose of Science is not to give us the ability to endure evil, but to give us dominion over evil.

In the fourth phase, we are not called upon to endure or out last dark and difficult trials, but to learn how to handle animal magnetism so effectively that we actually reduce it to nonexistence. When we can face evil, look into it and through it, and *know* that it is nothing, we are equipped with a form of divine intelligence that destroys it. Until we can exercise this power over it, we should not assume that we understand its nothingness, for evil is still present as a seemingly real and threatening force.

The price for learning evil's nothingness comes very high. Our warfare with it is long and hard, and the battle is most challenging at this particular time, for its resistance to being destroyed is strongest and most aggressive in the fourth phase.

The Subjective Handling of Animal Magnetism

We free consciousness of animal magnetism by handling it *subjectively. As* a rule, we tend to see all discord in our lives *objectively,* as coming through causes external to consciousness. We believe that our problems are from persons or circumstances outside of ourselves, and beyond our control.

But the handling of animal magnetism is totally subjective. Every form of discord is *hypnotic suggestion coming to you as a seeming reality.* If you reduce it to mesmerism and refuse to believe that the hypnotic illusion is real, you demonstrate dominion over it. *You must have an inner confrontation with your own solid conviction of evil's reality and fight against it until you conquer evil with your understanding of the truth.*

It is an awesome experience to go through the fourth phase and discover that you can be free of the claims of evil by handling them subjectively. You learn that, when evil is fearlessly resisted with your understanding of the truth, it collapses. It actually dissolves into nonexistence. It becomes nothing. This fact is proven by a consciousness spiritualized by Truth and Love, one that can stand unmoved by the most terrifying suggestions of evil, and fearlessly denounce them as illusions without power or reality. When you lose your fear of evil and can stand absolutely unintimidated by it, you have dominion over it, and it fades into oblivion.

By the time you reach the fourth phase, you already have had experience in handling animal magnetism through the treatment. You have learned that matter and mortality are subjective, and that evil seems to maintain its hold on you through mesmerism. Your demonstrations to this point have been invaluable preparation for dealing with the fourth phase.

Again and again, Mrs. Eddy writes of this internal struggle with evil that we are all destined to have. In *Retrospection and Introspection,* she says, "It is scientific to abide in conscious harmony, in health-giving, deathless Truth and Love. To do this, mortals must first open their eyes to all the illusive forms, methods, and subtlety of error, in order that the illusion, error, may be destroyed; if this is not done, mortals will become the victims of error."

Whether error comes from within through your own mortal traits and beliefs, or through aggressive mental suggestions from without, the struggle to destroy it remains subjective. Being subjective, you can choose whether you are going to allow animal magnetism to control your thought, or whether you are going to fight it out and demonstrate your control over it.

Evil's Unreality

So often the question is asked, Where does evil come from if it is not real? How can it be nothing when it seems so powerful? We do not find satisfying answers to these questions until we reach the fourth phase.

At this point, however, we must ask the *right* question. It is futile to try to explain what evil is and where it comes from. Instead, we need to ask, *How can I prove that evil is nothing?* That is the question.

Sometimes, in Christian Science, evil's unreality is compared to a mistake in mathematics which is easily corrected by supplying the right answer. This is an over- simplified and naive comparison. It is easy to correct a wrong answer in addition, for there is no resistance to our doing so. But animal magnetism so resists being destroyed that at times it seems more real and powerful than God.

Therefore, we should begin our demonstration over it by having absolute faith in Mrs. Eddy's statements regarding evil's nothingness. We must trust that she is right, and that our efforts to work from this premise will eventually enable us to prove what she teaches on this.

Christian Science is an education in spiritual things. It is a learning process through which spiritual lessons unfold in an orderly manner. These lessons appear to be increasingly difficult as we progress, just as algebra is more difficult than addition. These advanced lessons become more severe because animal magnetism is increasingly active in resisting its own destruction. A thorough understanding of evil's unreality comes only as we graduate from the fourth phase. But to see this lesson through is to achieve such an advanced form of intelligence that we never again feel totally at the mercy of evil.

Seeing Through Evil's Veil of Matter

Mrs. Eddy's insistence on the unreality of evil may create a conflict in consciousness between the seeming reality of evil and the spiritual fact of God's allness. This duality is due to the universal belief in evil. Before Christian Science is introduced into consciousness, evil seems so real and so powerful, that we come to accept all the claims of matter and mortal mind as inevitable. The entire structure of the human mind is built on the belief that evil and matter are a basic element in mortal existence. This view is the only one we have until we take up the study of Christian Science.

As Christian Science is introduced into consciousness, we have two views. Science also shows how to separate these two views — how to deny animal magnetism and demonstrate spiritual understanding.

As you work with the treatment, you learn to recognize the various beliefs of animal magnetism coming as specific claims. You also learn to handle false traits, and matter and its laws. With each phase, you gain experience in handling evil through spiritual, rather than human means. You begin to see that every negative thought is an illusion within your own mental atmosphere, and that it needs to be handled through the treatment and overcome subjectively. Through these phases, you press ever deeper into spiritual reality.

When you understand the unreality of matter, even to a small degree, you *begin to see through the facade that evil hides behind.* Consider carefully the fact that evil uses matter as a subterfuge, a means for camouflaging the origin of matter and mortality, which is animal magnetism itself

Until you discern the unreality of matter, animal magnetism goes unchallenged in your thinking, because you tend to handle the *effects* of evil, rather than evil itself. When you learn that there is no reality in matter — its only existence is your belief in it — the entire illusion of matter begins to crumble. The veil of matter that evil hides behind is dissolving.

So long as you believe in matter as real and blame all mortal conditions on mindless forces outside of consciousness, you never arrive at the actual cause of all discord — the *mesmeric influence of animal magnetism claiming to operate within consciousness as matter.* Do you believe that you depend on matter for your very existence? Do you blame sickness, disease, accidents, adversity, lack, age, death on material conditions? You surely do so constantly. You are conditioned to search for material causes for everything. In so doing, you never see beneath the surface of matter, and discern animal magnetism as the cause of mortal life. The belief in matter blinds you to the fact that mortal existence is a structure of mesmeric illusions originating in animal magnetism, imaged forth as matter.

When you begin to see that there is no matter, you are about to discover that all discord has its origin in the mesmeric suggestions of evil. If there is no material law, no material cause and effect, no material universe or man, then the discord in human experience must be coming from animal magnetism. Seeing this, you can look *through* the visible universe, and discern that the cause of discord is not matter, but animal magnetism. Then you can go straight to the cause in handling every claim — straight to animal magnetism itself! If you will face it and handle it until you lose your fear of it, you have dominion over it. Evil can no longer control you. In this fourth phase, you learn how to go beneath matter's seeming reality, identify evil's hypnotic influence, and destroy it through study and treatment.

In my experience, I considered the fourth phase the hardest lesson, for when you see through the illusion of matter, even to a small degree, evil knows its hidden influence over you is about to end, for the *next* step in your spiritual unfoldment is to see that evil is unreal. Therefore, it foams up and fights against its own destruction. Knowing its cloak of matter is gone, and that it is destined to lose its hold on you, it uses every means possible to put an end to your work.

I tell you about this phase, not to frighten you, but to help you understand what is happening when you reach the fourth phase in your work. Evidently everyone, sooner or later, must pass through this most difficult experience, and it is better to understand it, than to encounter it without knowing why it is taking place. It is usually easier to work through a difficult experience, if we know there is a good reason to do so.

During this phase, you must trust that God will give you the strength and courage to get through it. The only way you can learn to handle evil is through a long and difficult warfare with it in which you come out the victor.

When you have been so devoted to understanding God and have gone through the first three phases, you are tempted to resent the trials that come upon you in this phase. You feel you don't deserve them. Even though you apparently don't, you have them anyway, for it seems there is no other way to learn the lesson of evil's unreality. No two people go through this phase in exactly the same way. Yet everyone has to learn that God is all and that evil is nothing, and this internal warfare with the belief in evil appears to be the only way to learn it.

This difficult and prolonged lesson has been called the wilderness experience, the furnace of affliction, the burning of the tares, a dark night of the soul. At times it is, indeed, a night without a star.

The Warfare with Evil Illustrated

In my own experience, this warfare came upon me suddenly. I had worked for a very long time trying to resolve the seeming reality of matter. It was a challenging demonstration, but I had only my own thoughts to contend with. When the breakthrough came, it was a quiet, yet awesome, revelation.

Even though I had resolved the question of matter's unreality, I was aware that there was something more I had to learn. I felt I lacked the dominion necessary to resolve problems that my metaphysical work was still unable to overcome.

I was not aware at that time that my small insight into matter's unreality had stripped away evil's camouflage, and I would soon have to learn the unreality of evil itself. I later realized that this furnace experience was the next lesson in the overall plan — one that was the most important of all, and the most difficult.

Following my resolving of the illusion of matter, circumstances suddenly developed that seemed devastating. They swept away all the good I had accomplished. Misunderstandings and hatred developed in a number of my closest relationships. A change that had promised to be very progressive turned out to be a great disappointment. Also, for the first time, I began to see that the church organization, to which I was deeply devoted, was given more to politics and power struggles than to working for the good of the Cause. It was a very dark and confusing time.

I did not understand why these trials were happening to me. I had been faithfully working to make a better demonstration of Christian Science, only to be rewarded by defeat and disillusionment in almost all avenues of my personal life. The question kept arising, Why is this happening to me? Why am I suffering in spite of my best efforts to know God, while those around me are going along, blissful in their ignorance, untouched by such severe trials? Looking back, I realize that this experience was to teach me the unreality of evil.

Until we understand and prove evil's nothingness, it seems very real, very threatening, very powerful. When it cannot paralyze our progress in the earlier phases, and we reach the fourth phase, it comes at us through every opening it can find. And it comes with such force as to discourage us, destroy our faith in God, turn us against Mrs. Eddy, and make us give up Christian Science. When we understand that there is a reason for this trial, we press on to learn from it what it has to teach us.

When this anguishing set of circumstances came upon me, there was no human answer to them. They were irrevocable. There was no turning back time and returning things to their former state. Everything seemed black and hopeless.

Yet, I knew that there had to be a spiritual answer to this terrible ordeal, and a *spiritual* reason for it happening. As I prayed to find the answer, there came as a revelation a distinct separation between the real life "hid with Christ in God," and the mortal so-called life. On one side of this separation was the joy, warmth, intelligence, harmony, and perfection of divine Love. All that was good existed in this spiritual life, and it was very real and very tangible existence. Yet, it was separate, above and beyond mortal existence.

On the other side of this division was the discord, mis-understanding, loss, disappointment and despair of a mortal, mate-rial life, and this life was unreal. It claimed to originate in animal magnetism.

As this separation grew more distinct, I could place the disturbing experiences and my emotional reactions to them in the realm of the unreal and deny that this mortal experience had any intelligence, law, energy, power, or reality. I could say in the words of Christ Jesus, "Depart from me, I never knew you."

At the same time, I was able to withdraw into the spiritual sense of life, and see that God alone is real, that man has a perfect life intact and undisturbed in the divine Mind. Regardless of what takes place humanly, this spiritual life goes on in perfect harmony — untouched by the discord of mortal existence. This was the life God gave me.

With this separation of the real from the unreal, I found that I could put all forms of animal magnetism into the realm of the unreal, and with divine authority, I could turn on every claim and deny its seeming reality with such strength and conviction that it dissolved into nothingness. For the first time, my fear of evil began to lessen, and I was not so intimidated by its threatening sugges-tions, or the seeming reality of the discord taking place.

In this dark and lonely trial, I learned how to face animal magnetism — face it down, and reduce it to nothing. As I did this, I came out of the experience a very different person. I saw clearly the absolute separation between God and animal magnetism. My struggle with evil destroyed many ingrained and subtle forms of self-will, materialism, personal sense, fear, and emotionalism. It brought a spiritual peace I could not have found otherwise. I began to have dominion over evil. As hard as it was, the lesson was worth all that I had to go through in order to learn it. My metaphysical work became scientific, and many statements by Mrs. Eddy were illumined with new meaning. This terrible trial proved to be filled with blessings, and I have always been grateful for having gone through it.

My struggle with animal magnetism did not end with this initial insight into evil's unreality. There remained many problems to be solved, but for the first time I knew they were forms of animal magnetism that I could handle through the treatment. This on-going struggle continued for a very long time. With each new challenge, I withdrew into study and prayer, and fought it out with evil until I had reduced the problem to the hypnotic work of animal magnetism. Then I vehemently denied the mesmerism and affirmed the truth until I had dominion over the mesmerism and found healing.

Eventually, this work brought about another unexpected revelation. Although I could discern the unreality of matter and animal magnetism, I still had a mortal view of man. My mental image of others was one of mortal personalities. Then one day there began a very strange chemicalization in consciousness. The mortal concept was brought to the surface of consciousness and began to dissolve — leaving a strange void. For several weeks, this state of mind continued, and those around me seemed to have no mental depth. Then there unfolded in its place a spiritual dimension to man. It was as though I could look through the mortal personality of others and see beneath the outer self the presence of a spiritual selfhood, one with God.

This amazing insight into the real man brought a new view of everyone. There was a transparency to them. Whatever their human status, or present personality, I saw through it as though it were a mask, and sensed beneath and beyond it the indestructible selfhood in God's likeness. This spiritual relationship was indestructible. Whatever transpired humanly, this hidden image remained the real selfhood that would in time manifest itself as the individual's true identity. This selfhood was perfect, harmonious, the complete reflection of God. It could never be disturbed or destroyed. It was forever safe in God's keeping.

This unfoldment brought a great change in my attitude towards others. I found I didn't see their faults much any more. I wasn't even inclined to be judgmental, critical, unkind, or upset by anything they said or did, because I knew they were really the sons and daughters of God, and they would eventually outgrow the belief in a mortal existence.

I also came to see that each individual is God's responsibility. Each is held in His loving care; and his true identity, complete and perfect, would eventually become the only selfhood that he would express.

With this realization of man's likeness to God, my view of reality was, in some small way, complete. I saw the spiritual idea of man and the universe instead of the material view. It is difficult to explain what it is like to emerge into this very primitive — yet distinct — phase of spiritual consciousness. But it is a state of mind well worth striving for.

Although these revelations brought a better insight into reality, my severe struggle with animal magnetism in this phase continued for a very long time. As one problem was solved metaphysically, another seemed to take its place. But with each healing, my ability to detect and overcome animal magnetism improved. Then there came a time when a sense of peace filled my inmost thoughts. As this gentle peace remained, I knew this furnace experience had at last come to an end.

Understanding the Furnace Experience

Many good people go through experiences as severe as mine. The furnace experience is not unique. But when it comes upon us as we are working so diligently in Christian Science, it is hard to understand — unless we have some insight into animal magnetism and its reaction to our work in Science. We should be prepared for this ordeal in order to get through it.

Otherwise, we become like Job — perplexed at having such severe trials. We ask, "Why me?" for we seem not to deserve this dark and dreadful experience. But when we know that the experience comes to bless us, we can stand and absolutely trust that God will not let go of us. *During these dark times, we must not for one second doubt Mrs. Eddy's revelation nor neglect our study and the treatment, since they are the means for getting through this challenging phase.*

So long as evil seems real, we are going to be afraid of it, and so we remain in bondage to it, and suffer from believing in a power apart from God. Once our fear of evil has been broken and we are unintimidated by its mesmeric lies, we exercise ever-increasing dominion over it. We handle it as one having authority over it. We can separate it from person, place or thing, and destroy it metaphysically. Such work is quick, powerful, even instantaneous. This absolute conviction of evil's unreality is a major development in our work in Christian Science.

Evil's Aggression

The attacks of evil come in many ways — through undeserved abuse and hatred from others, from misunderstandings and unjust circumstances over which we seem to have no control, through loved ones who fail and reject us when we need them most, through loss of income, and through physical problems. In this fourth phase, it seems that animal magnetism tries to obstruct our progress through every human weakness it can find in us.

Whatever the challenges, however severe they may be, they are intended to make us lose our faith in Christian Science. Evil is working to destroy our spirituality, our inner rapport with God, because we are on the verge of understanding that it is nothing. When we do, it no longer controls us. We are in control of our own mind. The purpose of this fourth phase is to show us how to uncover and destroy evil fearlessly and completely in the heart of prayer.

When this furnace experience takes place, every human resource fails us. Money is useless. Human prestige, influence, and power are nothing. Rationalization, intellect, education and experience are worthless. The self-will, human planning, and drive, which we may have used in the past, prove futile. Even the metaphysical work that had been successful does not help us. When we pray as before, nothing happens. As the furnace gets hotter, we are forced to yield up every human thing and rely completely on God for help. Even then, evil seems so real, so overwhelming at times, that we doubt our ability to overcome it. Yet if we endure, if we continue to study and pray, if we learn what God is teaching us, we will overcome our fear of evil.

The Ultimate Breakthrough

When, for the first time, you stand in the face of evil's most hateful attack and press on as best you can, never giving up, never admitting defeat, and at the darkest hour standing alone with God, refusing to doubt Him, you will realize a turning point — and evil will collapse. It will actually dissolve into nothingness. This is a great revelation, an awesome discovery. In a sense, it is the ultimate breakthrough. You begin to understand how evil can be reduced to nonexistence through prayer alone. Never again will evil seem so intimidating as to make you believe it is real. Each time you hold your ground, endure the suffering, and work on, you will find that evil can be made to disappear into nothingness.

When taking this stand, you learn how to turn on evil and fight against it until you feel the hypnotic suggestions weaken and give out. In each battle with it, you will sense a turning point in which your strength and power is greater than the mesmeric suggestion. Using this mental strength to banish the suggestion, you will feel it weaken, give way, and fade out of consciousness. And so you prove that God, good, is a presence and power greater than evil. This conviction is so absolute that you can from then on face evil and handle it with such authority that you can defeat it.

This is the astonishing and unexpected result of your battle with evil. When you turn and fight it, rather than run from it, it collapses into nonexistence. It is no longer there! If you refuse to stop praying, mesmeric suggestions, seemingly so real, so ominous, begin to weaken. They gradually dissolve until they disappear. If you will not admit they are real, if you stand and refuse to believe that they have any power, they fade away. Then you know that evil is nothing but a bluff, an illusion, an unreality. Indeed, evil is nothing!

The Challenge of the Furnace Experience

Mrs. Eddy once told her mental workers, "Hold on and persist for good, because there never is a hopeless situation. When error meets with resistance, it begins to be scattered. Where a situation seems unbearable, it is because error is letting go." This statement sums up the demonstration over evil.

During this furnace experience, our human life is shaken to the core. It becomes bleak, empty, discordant, almost unbearable. And so we are forced to press through the unreal mental images within and find to some small degree our oneness with God. And it is there!

When this wilderness experience follows upon the discovery that matter is unreal, you must realize that you have not failed in your work. Indeed, you have been so successful that you have entered a new phase of the work. Evil is threatened to the core. It is about to become unreal to you, and so it stops at nothing in keeping you from this ultimate breakthrough. After passing through this Armageddon, you have a form of divine intelligence that you could not have attained in any other way.

In this fourth phase of your journey, the trials you face may be many. You may overcome one challenge, only to find it followed by another just as difficult. Each trial must be resolved metaphysically. In this phase, you learn that in the mortal realm, evil is not nothing. It is an unmerciful force with a black and bitter hatred of the Christ-consciousness. It is sadistic. It inflicts pain and suffering on mankind without conscience. It is at its worst when its hold on the mind is threatened. And so we cannot say evil is nothing — until we can prove it is nothing.

In the spiritual realm, evil is nothing. Through an understanding of Christian Science and the prayer of affirmation and denial, you can face evil fearlessly, reverse its hypnotic suggestions, and reduce it to what it really is — absolutely nothing! You can refuse to consent to the aggressive mental suggestions of evil. You can de-mesmerize consciousness, and prove again and again the unreality of mortality and matter. Each time you deal with a problem as hypnotic suggestion coming from animal magnetism, rather than a bad relationship, or lack, or a physical claim, you strengthen your ability to control evil and put it out.

The purpose of Christian Science is not to make us comfortable in a material life, but to so educate us in spiritual things that we begin to have dominion over all forms of evil. Only then are we safe from its malicious control and the suffering it brings. This requires that we face the mesmerism that evil puts forth and lose our fear of it. We then reach a point where we remain unmoved, uninfluenced, untouched by evil at all times and under all circumstances. As we reduce the hypnotic suggestions to nothing, we learn that there is no power in evil to limit or harm us.

When I was learning this very hard lesson, there was a simple little story that summed up this battle with evil. There was a dog that was always chasing a poor little cat. Day and night the dog gave the cat no peace. Then one day the cat couldn't run any longer. It was exhausted, and so in desperation it turned, arched its back, and hissed at the dog, and the dog turned and ran.

When you turn on animal magnetism — at times out of desperation and exhaustion — and decide to fight it out with evil, when you refuse to submit to its lies any longer, you can realize a victory over it.

In the battle with evil, you struggle mentally with the on-slaught of hypnotic suggestions until you reverse them, see through them, and replace them with the truth of being. The more you do this, the easier it becomes. You come to see that evil has no power except what you give it.

This new-found ability to handle evil so effectively revolu-tionizes your healing work. You know as fact — not theory — that evil has no power or reality. You develop the strength and under-standing to battle with it. In fact, I believe God does not bring us into this advanced lesson until we are ready for it. Mrs. Eddy writes of this in *Science and Health,* "If good enough to profit by Jesus' cup of earthly sorrows, God will sustain us under these sorrows."

Using   Metaphysics — Not Human Means

If we are going to demonstrate dominion over evil, it has to be done subjectively. We cannot use human means or will-power for resolving these challenges. When this testing time comes, we must have the courage and strength to stand and face evil down — *metaphysically.* There is always the temptation to deal with adver-sity in a human way. But the lesson in these trials is to teach us that evil is nothing. We must understand this fact, not merely believe it. In this phase of our work, we should not resort to human means for resolving our difficulties. Instead, we must withdraw into the closet, face each crisis or challenge, and fight it out with animal magnetism until we are free of its hypnotic suggestions. We do this by destroying its power to make us afraid of it.

Rather than give up in despair when things seem black, you can decide that each trial is an opportunity to prove your power over evil. Then stand! No matter what the outer picture seems to be presenting, refuse to believe that evil is true or real. Decide that you will fight it out on the mental battle field until evil gives out. Then continue to do so until you feel its hypnotic attack weaken and begin to fade away. At that point, work on with even greater determination, and you will have your healing

When Problems Worsen

Sometimes when you work like this, the problem seems to grow worse. And so it may appear that your work is not being effective. Actually, the very opposite is taking place. When your work is successfully destroying evil, its resistance becomes so intense that the problem seems to worsen, and you may believe that you cannot meet it. This is what evil wants you to believe. Therefore, this is the very time when you need to work the hardest, for the work is being so effective that it is forcing evil's resistance to the limit. When you out last it and work on regardless of the outer picture, evil's resistance to your work gives out, the problem will yield, and healing will follow.

The purpose of this phase is to teach you that evil collapses into nothing if you resist it with the truth understood. No matter how ominous or overwhelming it may seem to be, evil is nothing but hypnotic suggestion, and any hypnotic spell can be broken through dedicated metaphysical work.

Relying on the Law of Love

Throughout this phase, animal magnetism will strike most often through personal relationships. We are most vulnerable through those we care most about — family, friends, relatives, neighbors, business and social acquaintances. When our most difficult challenges come through persons, our demonstration of the law of Love enables us to get through such times. If animal magnetism attacks us most aggressively through our relationships — especially those nearest and dearest to us — and we take it personally, we can become so emotionally involved that we cannot impersonalize the problem and handle it as mesmerism. If we have not mellowed enough to be forgiving, patient, kind, and compassionate towards those causing the discord, if we see misunderstandings and abuse as a personal confrontation between two people, then we react with hatred, revenge, hurt feelings, anger, disappointment, and so on. This reaction can make such a reality of the problem that we are unable to handle it metaphysically.

When we impersonalize these experiences and analyze them in the light of Christian Science, we see through the persons and circumstances, and recognize animal magnetism as using others to attack us. It does not matter through whom, or for what reason, the confrontation or abuse comes, it is ultimately animal magnetism using these different minds to attack and destroy us. Knowing this, we have a correct analysis of what is happening. We can maintain control of our thoughts and emotions, and handle each challenge competently and scientifically. In this way we begin to demonstrate our control over animal magnetism when it uses such channels against us.

We need to impersonalize the error and remain loving toward those who seem to be persecuting us. We cannot react in a personal way. Christ Jesus, before Pilate, "opened not his mouth." He did not react, but rather saw through those hating and mocking him, to animal magnetism attacking him, trying to destroy his Christ-consciousness. Instead of having a heated confrontation with the people abusing him, he said nothing to inflame their hatred. He was loving, even to the healing of the soldier's ear, which Peter had cut off. His compassion for those who persecuted him was his salvation, for it enabled him to rise above the malicious animal magnetism, impersonalize evil, and overcome it. Christ Jesus maintained dominion over evil's attack, because he did not take it personally.

In the same way, when we find ourselves under personal attack, we can come through this hard lesson if we obey the law of Love. If we remain loving toward those causing our difficulties, we are then able to handle the error impersonally and deal with it metaphysically, rather than through confrontations.

What good is it to react personally to such situations? Our work in Christian Science is subjective. We must fight mentally with aggressive mental suggestions, rather than with persons. We must deny and reject evil again and again, look straight at it until we are totally unintimidated by it, and refuse to be overcome by it. In so doing, we overcome error with Truth and Love. Mrs. Eddy's works provide us with instructions for doing this, for she understood so well this internal struggle with evil. When we handle unjust personal attacks metaphysically, they gradually disappear.

Following the Example of Others

Whatever your individual trials in the hard struggle with evil, take heart in the fact that others before you have entered the furnace of affliction, gone through it, and come out on the other side. With Christian Science, you can also endure this experience and learn the awesome lesson that evil is nothing.

Unfortunately, you will not clear out the whole of animal magnetism through one hard-fought battle. You will continue to have struggles with it indefinitely. But the fourth phase teaches you how to turn on evil and resist it until it collapses. *Then you know that God is all and evil is nothing.*

The all-out struggle with evil is the hardest of our spiritual lessons, mainly because we do not understand why we are experiencing it. But once we have worked through it and know how to handle evil, future struggles are not as hard, because we know how to reduce the discord to hypnotic illusion and destroy it through study and treatment.

This fourth phase marks a great turning point in the demonstration of your oneness with God. Following this hard struggle with animal magnetism, you enter the fifth phase and glimpse spiritual reality.

FIFTH PHASE: ENTERING THE SECRET PLACE

It is impossible to describe the lightness, happiness, and peace which follow the furnace experience. First of all, there is the stunning realization that *the universe and man are spiritual, and that God is All*. You find that Mrs. Eddy is right in every statement she has made about God and man. And you have been right in having faith in her revelation. The immortal words of John sum up this first emergence into light: "And I saw a new heaven and a new earth: for the first heaven and first earth had passed away; and there was no more sea."

When the material view is the only one we have, we cannot visualize the end result if we should give up a material sense of existence for the spiritual. There is the fear that, as the material dissolves, there is nothing to replace it. When the mind is void of matter and a mortal sense of life, this suggests a vacuum within, because we seem totally dependent on matter and mortal mind for our very existence. It is the only structure of thought we have ever known. In this single material viewpoint, everyone seems encased in a material form, at the mercy of material laws, and a victim of animal magnetism. The material world seems so real that we cannot imagine another reality as tangible and visible as the images comprising mortal existence. It would seem that as matter and mortality disappear — we would lose everything.

But this does not happen. As we pass through these phases, we learn that we do not destroy our life or our world. *We translate them into spiritual ideas.* We add a spiritual dimension to the universe, and see all things as they really are — ideas in the one Mind, expressions of the infinite One.

Christ Jesus said, "Whoso loseth his life for my sake shall find it." Thus, we lose the mortal sense of life and discover our true life hidden in the secret place. *Science and Health* states, "Metaphysics resolves things into thoughts, and exchanges the objects of sense for the ideas of Soul."

After we have gone through the fourth phase, we have a new view of things. The outer world remains the same. Seasons come and go. Flowers bloom. Snow falls. There are sunny days and starry nights. Life goes on. But inwardly we see everything in a new light. Our subjective view of creation and man is now beginning to include a touch of divine reality. All things have a transparency as we see through the visible universe and discern behind it the divine Principle, Love.

Material images are seen to be only illusions in the mind. The darkness which blinded us to the real universe and man gives way to spiritual light. The mist of matter thins out. Fear of animal magnetism lessens. The spiritual viewpoint unfolds, transforming the universe into a new place. God becomes a pulsating, thinking Mind, creating and sustaining all things, working out all events large and small. God is intimately involved in planning and caring for all that transpires in the spiritual universe, down to the smallest detail. He is All-in-all.

With this emergence into light, we begin to visualize reality as it really is — a perfect, harmonious manifestation of divine intelligence and love. Although the spiritual nature of reality is only faintly discerned at this point, the separation of the material and spiritual viewpoints is more distinct than it has ever been, and at times the spiritual is more dominant than the material.

There is no matter in the spiritual realm, for every atom is created and controlled by God. Not one atom in the whole of creation can be separated from the love and intelligence that governs it. "All things are created spiritually," Mrs. Eddy tells us. If atomic structure and behavior are of God, then underlying all things is the spiritual realm of Mind. Mind is cause and creation is effect. They are inseparable, and there is no matter in this oneness. Where before things appeared to be opaque, hard, material objects, they now begin to take on the fourth dimension of Spirit.

There is no evil in this heavenly place. Every thought and feeling reflects love, for the divine Principle, Love, governs all. In the whole of creation there is not one negative thought or emotion. Everything is the expression of divine Love.

The laws originating and governing reality are of God. Therefore, the universe is seen to be a creation of beauty and goodness. No one is at the mercy of matter and its laws. Evil does not impose suffering, disease, limitation, and death on the real universe and real man. All things reflect unity, harmony and perfection.

Great freedom and joy become ours when we emerge from the long, hard struggle with animal magnetism into this new realm of Love, and discover that we are living in the spiritual universe. We have always lived in it. There is no other universe beyond it or above it, nowhere else to go, no other place to be. Look around you, for you are in the universe of God's creating. This is it! You are in heaven, for earth becomes heaven, when you learn to see it as the spiritual creation it is.

True being exists intact and undisturbed in the spiritual realm. It is above and beyond the mortal dream of life in matter, untouched by animal magnetism. As God is one with the atoms and stars, so is He one with man. Here and now, we are inseparable from Him. Knowing this, we can demonstrate everything that takes place in our daily life by relating all things to God, Mind, rather than to animal magnetism. To the degree that we understand that our experiences — down to the smallest detail — take place in Mind, not matter, we find that the harmony and perfection governing the universe also govern our being.

We inhabit the universe of God's creating. God is the Father and Mother of all, and each individual is one with Him. God establishes our place and holds us in it. He anticipates our every need, and provides the channels through which He unfolds our good to us.

Every individual, regardless of his human situation and background, is the son or daughter of God. Since he lives in the spiritual universe, he must always be one with the Father. Above and beyond his mortal personality, his real life and identity remain indestructible and perfect in the one Mind. Everyone is safe in God's keeping.

It is an awesome experience to glimpse the secret place where God is All-in-all. Mrs. Eddy writes in *Science and Health* of "the Christ, Truth, hidden in sacred secrecy from the visible world." She also tells us, "Christians rejoice in secret beauty and bounty, hidden from the world, but known to God." To be able to explore this hidden realm and live in its "secret beauty and bounty" should be the ultimate goal of our work in Christian Science.

Once we come through the fourth phase, we enter a very elementary form of spiritual consciousness. It would be misleading for me to tell you that this is the end of your work. Your adventure into the spiritual realm is just beginning. The warfare with animal magnetism is not over. Far from it. But from this time on, you understand this on-going battle with evil and how to win it. Although you can not as yet totally prove evil's unreality, you know how it can be done. It is essential that you continue to study Christian Science and work with the treatment. In studying the Scriptures and Mrs. Eddy's works, absolute statements about God and man become increasingly clear and logical. All that she is trying to tell you falls into place. The treatment is filled with healing power. And the world you live in is governed more by divine intelligence, wisdom and love, than by mortal belief. The purpose of study and treatment now is to make the structure of the spiritual realm as concrete and real as the material now seems to be.

The struggle with animal magnetism continues, but with each victory, the vision of divine reality is more clearly defined. Your place in the spiritual realm becomes established and secure. You develop a oneness with God that cannot be taken from you.

The divine plan is so deep and complex an experience that this discussion is no more than a bare outline of it. But having defined the five phases, you can now think about them and use them as a guide in going from the mortal to the immortal. You can begin demonstrating your oneness with God.

The Blessings Found in Demonstrating the Divine Plan.

Why should you undertake such a long and difficult demonstration of Christian Science? Because the blessings that flow from this advanced spiritual understanding are beyond anything that could be humanly planned and achieved.

Mrs. Eddy once outlined to her students the changes that could come about when they give up a material life for the spiritual. She wrote:

> *We must cease quibbling, cease to admit in our thinking the reality and power in themselves, of misery, pain, and evil in all its forms. We must think steadily and persistently the Truth which stands opposite to them. We do in this way overcome our discordant conditions of consciousness.*
>
> *Now, everyone that persists in this course, several times a day, will have the following signs, viz,:*
>
> *1st. Signs of lessening fear of aught that can happen to them.*
>
> *2d. Signs of mental equilibrium, a self-poise and reliance that faces steadily that which others flee from.*

73

*3d. Lack of painful consequences from
doing that which is one's duty to do.*

*4th. Signs of less love for those things
which we formerly considered necessary for our
happiness, a growing independence of them*

*5th. Broadening love and charity, en-
circling around that which is ours, and includ-
ing all men.*

*6th. Strength sufficient for the demand
of each day, when each day's work only is considered,*

*7th. Signs of peace within which all the
tempests of mortal belief cannot destroy — a
"Holy of Holies" with ever-burning lamp; a
covenant with God, the All-good; the peace
which passeth all understanding; a peace which
is above and beyond happiness.*

This list shows that the work is not one of endless toil and
struggle, trials and tribulation. The good that flows from a demonstration of the divine plan is beyond describing. Our progress through
the five phases has a dramatic effect on our personal life. As
revelations of truth unfold, they reach to the very heart of consciousness and renovate the inmost thoughts and feelings. They
bring irrevocable changes in how we think.

As consciousness is spiritualized, our whole being is
affected. We have many unexpected healings. The changed mental atmosphere moves forth effortlessly and heals the outer life.
Actually, it pours blessing upon blessing into our experience. Many
of these blessings are unplanned, unexpected gifts from God. We
have no way of knowing what they are going to be. They are the
result of our realization of Truth. As our thinking improves, our
human situation improves. The inner change and outer change move
forward together.

As we move deeper into Christian Science, we find healings take place naturally, effortlessly, without necessarily doing specific work to bring them about.

Our health is better because many mortal traits and beliefs which cause sickness and age have been replaced with spiritual qualities. In living the law of Love, we prevent the illness produced by hate, fear, self-will. If we become ill, we work to find the mental or emotional cause for it. Thus we gradually put out of consciousness the causes of sickness, disease and age.

We learn to handle the fear of lack and to demonstrate a better sense of supply, in which we rely on God for all things. The more we trust Him to care for us, the better our sense of supply.

We are protected from accidents, catastrophes, disasters, things going wrong, confusion, chaos, forgetting or misplacing or losing things. Endless little aggravations cease. Instead, we find things going well, things always working out for us. There is peace, orderliness, an almost effortless sense of daily activity.

Our relationships reflect more harmony and love. As we progress spiritually, difficult, demanding, aggravating relationships either become harmonious or come to an end. Incompatible people drift out of our lives, often without any confrontation or animosity. As we demonstrate our relationships, we are freed of those who are hostile towards Christian Science.

We find that many materialistic, selfish, or worldly pursuits and interests leave us, for we outgrow them. A different kind of life unfolds — one that is God-centered rather than world-centered. We think and live in a different dimension of mind than the material world around us. In a sense, we begin to *be* spiritual man.

We are able to protect ourselves against aggressive mental suggestion and malicious malpractice. As consciousness becomes increasingly enlightened through divine unfoldment, we can detect whether we are thinking our thoughts, God's thoughts, or another's thoughts. Knowing this, we can defend ourselves from malicious malpractice.

We learn the Science and art of healing through prayer alone. When we understand how to separate animal magnetism from person and handle it as impersonal error, we can heal with great assurance. Our prayerful work is no longer guesswork. It is more than faith in Christian Science. We know how to attack and destroy the seeming cause of a claim. Knowing this, our healing work is extremely effective.

Through each phase of our unfoldment, we develop a better rapport with God. As we struggle with the seeming reality of animal magnetism and overcome it, the belief in evil dies out, and so do many false traits — fear, anger, hate, resentment, personal sense, self-will, envy, jealousy, to name a few. The furnace experience drains us of the heaving sea of mortal emotions and brings a calmness and peace "which passeth all understanding." As false emotions disappear, our true selfhood, hidden within, comes forth to fill the void. Spiritual intuitions replace human intellect and reason. When we listen more to God and less to ourselves, we are sensitive to the "still small voice" of Truth and Love. When we hear this voice, there is a feeling of being at one with God. We move with God's inner promptings. As we learn to obey these intuitions, we demonstrate all that we do.

We also learn that we do not change the world; we leave it, That is, we move ever deeper into the universe of Soul and leave behind the world of personal sense and materialism, with the experiences, relationships, and conditions that we once called life. Thinking is focused less and less on persons, and more and more on God.

We do not make a great sacrifice of worldly things and get nothing in return. Through a continued study of Science, many statements in Mrs. Eddy's works take on a depth and meaning which carry us far beyond any human interpretation of them. The presence and power of God become more real than the presence and power of evil.

Helping the World

Our world is going through a great chemicalization as a spiritual age dawns. Humanity is in dire need of healing and enlightenment — a need that Christian Science alone can supply. It is our responsibility to do all we can to meet this need, but we can do so only if we understand Christian Science. We cannot heal the world through blind faith in Truth. We must be able to prove this Science with healing works.

This does not necessarily mean that we should become practitioners, taking patients and charging fees. The very presence of the Christ, Truth, active in consciousness, radiates out to heal and transform world thought. Each time we exercise dominion over evil in our own experience, we do so for all mankind.

"One with God is a majority." Consider the everlasting effects that Christ Jesus had on the world by coming forth from the tomb, triumphant over death. And consider that Mrs. Eddy's discovery of the spiritual nature of man and the universe changed the course of history. Each one who shares in this revelation is making the greatest contribution possible to the healing of a troubled world. There is no way to measure the spiritualizing effect this prayerful work has on others. With such vision, it is possible to perform healing works comparable to those of Christ Jesus and Mrs. Eddy. As healings multiply, we will usher in the millennium.

Mrs. Eddy tells us, "We live in an age of Love's divine adventure to be All-in-all." We each have our place and purpose in this "divine adventure." As you demonstrate a more advanced understanding of Christian Science, God will unfold to you your own spiritual destiny. He will give meaning and direction to the new life that develops through your study of Christian Science. As you awake to your oneness with God, you will find that you have always been in His loving care.

ABOUT THE AUTHOR: Ann Beals is a life-long Christian Scientist. Her family came into Christian Science through a healing she had before she was a year old. Doctors could not diagnose the illness or cure it. She seemed about to pass on when her mother called in a Christian Science practitioner who prayed for her until she regained consciousness. Within a short time she was completely healed. Her parents then took up the study of Christian Science and the family attended First Church of Christ, Scientist in Louisville, Kentucky. During her early years she had several healings of extremely serious illnesses through reliance on Christian Science. In time her father, Harry Smith, became a Christian Science teacher and lecturer.

While attending Washington University in St. Louis, Missouri, Ms. Beals met and married Robert Beals. She has two sons, Charles and John. After serving the branch church in Decatur, Georgia, in many ways, she became a Christian Science practitioner, listed in *The Christian Science Journal*. She also contributed a number of articles to the Christian Science periodicals.

Early in her practice work, she realized the need for writings that explained more fully how to demonstrate Christian Science. But when she submitted deeper articles to the editors of the periodicals, they were unwilling to publish them.

As she watched the steady decline of the Christian Science Church, her concern for the future of the movement led her, in 1974, to publish independently of the Church organization her booklet *Animal Magnetism*. Because of Church policy, members of the Church, and especially *Journal* listed practitioners, were forbidden to publish writings without the permission of the Christian Science Board of Directors. After publishing her booklet, she was forced to resign her *Journal* listing as a practitioner.

In 1975, she met Reginald G. Kerry. He shared her deep concern about the decline in the Church. His work at Church headquarters in Boston had led him to see that the decline in the Church was largely due to the immorality and corruption at Church headquarters. He delivered an ultimatum to the Board of Directors that they either "clean up things at headquarters" or he would write Church members exposing the corruption and immorality there. When the Board refused to take his threat seriously, he carried out his promise to "write the field." Ms. Beals assisted him in sending the Kerry Letters. For two years, while living in Boston, she worked with him in getting out the first four Kerry Letters. Her book, *Crisis in the Christian Science Church*, tells of these events.

After mailing the fourth Kerry Letter, she moved to California. She resigned from the Church in 1977. She continued assisting the Kerrys in sending out the Letters. In 1980, she started The Bookmark with the conviction that the time had come when deeper writings on Christian Science had to be published and made available to everyone. As this work has progressed, she has been able to publish and promote many profound works on Christian Science that have been suppressed by the Board of Directors over the years.

She presently lives in Santa Clarita, California, where she continues to write papers on Christian Science, and serve as publisher and editor of The Bookmark.

For further information regarding Christian Science:
Write: The Bookmark
Post Office Box 801143
Santa Clarita, CA 91380
Call: 1-800-220-7767
Visit our website: www. thebookmark.com